Golden Gremlin

A Vigorous Push from Misanthropes and Geezers

Rod A. Walters

Omega Man Press   Ⓜ   Rochester, NY

"What good is your experience, if you can't help someone else with it?"
-author

Golden Gremlin
by Rod A. Walters

Publication © 2015, 2016
Omega Man Press
www.ieWriter.com

ISBN: 97809841792-0-6
ISBN: 09841792-0-8

When you hear the word *golden*, you are either a senior, or standing in front of a Chinese restaurant. If both, then step inside and get a great meal. If you're smart, you'll get a discount.

To Pop, the ultimate savvy senior.

Printed in the United States of America.

CONTENTS

CONTENTS

A WORD ABOUT BUSINESS

CONTENTS

CONTENTS

INTRODUCTION:
Publisher Scuffles

"I may be old, but I ain't dead."
- B.B. King

Part I: Poppy

H ave you ever heard of one of those older gents making a break for it from his Assigned Senior Residence Center (old folk's home)? If a determined old buzzard really needs to visit his publisher, then he might have to make some drastic moves. Like in this true story. Silly old man.

Part II: Testing the Limits

T he mower's electric starter fired up as smoothly as a blowtorch poking through a giant butter sculpture of Millard Fillmore. No official at the Center would notice the hubbub because their unreliable landscaping company mowed the grounds at odd times.

You see, the old gent had to go meet with his publisher, face to face, and the Center would under no circumstance let him drive their new company Mazda. Their gas-powered mower, therefore, would do just fine. At 11 mph top speed, it would take only a long, but leisurely half day to reach the publisher's office in the next town. He would be taking the back two-lane road through a bit of country.

Two jerry cans of gasoline strapped to the back of the mower would be plenty of fuel for the trip. A sack of assorted nonperishable eats nabbed from the past week's meals at the Center would be enough to get through the next day or so, and that case of C-store bottled water stashed behind the front seat by the landscaping company was an unexpected bonus. Anyway, the publisher was always good for a stiff drink or two and a hearty snack after he got there.

A local cop could pose an unexpected danger, stopping the old guy as he motored along the shoulder of the back road. Planning for this random kink in his plan, he practiced lowering and raising the mower blade deck many times, so to pretend he was busy tending to the weed growth on the shoulder. The movements had to look smooth. No point in hurrying, because the fresh air and the scenery were unsurpassed. Why, he might even make a few bucks by mowing some small farmer's front yard on the way. He would turn over any such earnings to the Center for the gas and mower rental costs. In the end, this old shoe was a fair guy.

Breakfast time arrived at the Center. The director casually asked no one in particular, "Where's Poppy?"

Part III: Scuffling with the Publisher

"Y ou have any trouble getting here, Poppy?" asks the publisher.

"Nope. I cut a few corners on the way, but I putt-putted into town all right," the old geezer casually flips back.

"Find a place to park okay?" continues the considerate publisher.

"Yup. I found a grassy spot and chained the beast to a birch tree," sez he.

The publisher, used to his client's odd ways, works hard *not* to roll his eyes, and then brings the talk around to important business. "All right Poppy, you say you came up with this great title for your book: 'Geezer.' We're going to go one better," sez the professional publisher, now warming to his own brilliance, "we want to title the book, 'Mein Geezer'."

"'Mein Geezer'?! You want to name the book 'Mein Geezer'?!" Poppy splutters, in shock, and not sure if this pro has all his croutons in the right salad bowl. Then waving his arms around like some kind of clumsy, inarticulate boob, he presses this genius, "You remember that guy in the 1920s with that ridiculous little moustache who wrote Mein Krampkopf, or something like that? And if my memory does well by me, I don't think Mr. Mein Krampfkopf had a very good end."

"BUT," sez the publisher, knowing he has his client on defense, "you'll admit that in round numbers, that book sold zillions, and old *Krampkopf* lasted another couple decades. Surely, Poppy, you have a good 20 years ahead of you?" sez this scoundrel slyly.

"But .... but...." sez the older man, still trying to get airborne with both arms. Cicero, he's not.

They sort of end the day with the publisher first mouthing slowly and dreamily at the ceiling, "'Mine Geezer,' 'Mein Geezer,' hmmm," then turning sternly and pointing a chubby finger, "Sometimes you act like an uninvited *gremlin* at a white-glove party, Poppy. Listen to me, and you'll be *golden*. And anybody tell you that you look like some kind of clumsy, inarticulate boob flapping your arms around like that?

"By the way, you will not need to write up a *query letter*, as we will be publishing your book. How about if I ride home with you in your car, and we can cut through the details on the way?"

"Poppy" has chosen to narrate the following tales, wisdom, true truths and assorted facts, except when someone else chooses to. The old geezer and his buddies make sense, most of the time, even when embellishing.

A Great Query Letter to Next Publisher

Dear Mr. BigBooks:

Anyone peddling a book about wise-aleck seniors, titled <u>Golden Gremlin,</u> would likely start a query letter with a clever and snorty sort of opening, though not to you, anyway. This bad idea will *not* get you to read the rest, and you are too important for all that. So, let us get started with the standard three-part query:

1. The Book
2. The Bloke
3. The Hook

    <u>Golden Gremlin: A Vigorous Push from Misanthropes and Geezers</u> got written to make Dave Barry and Ben Stein laugh. Remember, Dave Barry lives in Miami surrounded by seniors, and Ben Stein *is* one. The approximate word count, 49,600, is written to read quickly. The book consists of about 80 bite-sized pieces, to be consumed as easily as Henry VIII could with a large sack of candy-corns. I have attached a list of Contents titles for all these short pieces.
    Turning from a semi-lucrative engineering career to writing also turned my life upside down, or at least tilted everything with a 55° sideways list. It also turned me into the first card-carrying *golden gremlin*. That created enough fun to make plenty of material for this finger-poking book.
    <u>Golden Gremlin</u> divided itself early on into five life topic areas, ending with a self-proving coda. I made up that last phrase, but have found that people catch on

quickly to its meaning—the book finishes with spiky essays (plus a few inappropriate songs) to bind up and settle the first sections, and which punch and poke fun at the world. I earned this right with plenty of practice as a punching bag. Those first five topics deal with nature, words, business, food and kitchens, and history. What more could one ask for!

Since a healthy fraction of the 40+ million seniors in the USA almost surely see themselves as golden gremlins too, I plan to stalk AARP and AMAC. Being a member of both organizations, and in good standing, my presentations at both are assured. "Preaching to the choir" works well when the choir is really large, with hands on fat wallets and eye sights almost like mine.

Imagine a book signing at one of those great organizations. I place my stash of Golden Gremlins smack behind a table loaded with assorted cookies. A couple of young, friendly ushers can be hired to help with crowd control.

Thank you so much, and I do look forward to talking with you about this book. I promise to remember to mark down our date before I forget, then stick the note inside the refrigerator for safety.

Sincerely,

Rod A. "Poppy" Walters

AN UNEVEN HISTORY OF NATURE

Abracadumbell

A las, if only one of those good lamp genies could swoop down and wave his wand and make you instantly smarter. Yes, yes, you might want to wish for other swag, but Genie's one-time deal here is *twice smarter*. Be grateful.

There is another way to accomplish exactly the same thing, though, and I wish readers would think this one through.

What if the good genie would instead make everyone else two times *dumber* than you? Wave the wand, and POOF! The world around you gets less clever by half, as our British cousins say. Why is this dumbed down genie-miracle so great?

Consider some advantages. For huge example, you would *not* have to read more books at double speed. Just keep your same skills and routines. Everyone else's reading speed takes a dive. Relatively speaking, you now read twice as fast as they do. This includes *all* the Mr. Smarty speed-reader population.

You would also get *richer* for pretty much the same reason, though you would have to wait a little longer. You can harvest a little *dumb* money here and there, but sales still have to be made in quantity, bank accounts transferred, etc., all of which takes time. *Smarts* will not cut down much time on dumb stuff like that. Relatively speaking you make your bundle faster than the others with no more effort than "usual."

Relatively speaking, you already knew you were smarter than your relatives.

Like all good plans, you will have to weigh a couple of possible bad parts. Right away you must be prepared for the genie's balking at multiple wand-waves. For everyone else to get dumber, the genie likely needs to teleport to each continent separately to complete his waving duties. A genie who balks might become an irritated genie. Uh, oh. Also, in the confusion *you* might be the one who gets dumb-waved, and your bozo cousin gets auto-smarted. Relatively speaking, this is *not* good.

For another thing, being double-smarter will not get you around the grocery store faster. Although you plan your itinerary as well as before, everyone else in the store has gotten one-half dumber, and the aisles will clog up. See, dumber grocery shoppers will take longer to figure out unit prices. More likely, they will confuse the prices with expiration dates, blocking traffic badly as they bend over their diagonally parked shopping carts, open-mouthed breathing, trying to do the math.

In your own business, where we have just seen how you become richer than you would have been without this fabulous miracle, your now dumber customers or clients will be slower to pay. They will confuse the top and the bottom of your invoice, and often end up paying you the page number. This raises the serious risk of your going bust. Try to get them to pay your phone number instead, so make that figure in large, bold print at the top.

Oh, did I mention the price of this wand-waving miracle? Yes, you do get SuperSaver shipping, but you have to trade a body part—genie's choice—for the favor. At last report, he was collecting lower and lower. Something to consider.

Pals

Y ou know how, when you're driving down a double-lane city road and this kid zooms by, no signal light and guns it past you with baseball cap on? Backwards. Then good things happen. The traffic light turns red ahead of him, and both of you have to stop for the red light. There you are, side by side, you coming to a leisurely stop, him seething his buns off. We call this situation, Red Light Pals. Life gets extremely satisfying when the same thing happens at the next light, and the next, and the next.

CURE FOR THE RED LIGHT PALS SYNDROME: none, but at one of the stops you can flash your Red Light Pal one of those big, bright two-plus-dozen-tooth Cheshire grins.

Next, you're minding your own sweet business, driving on a regular divided highway, at the speed limit and controlled by your trusty cruise control. In the right lane. Then this geezer with a flat hat somehow pulls up behind you at wolf-at-the-neck distance from your rear end and stays there. This gent probably doesn't mean to be a royal (and dangerous) pain in the fundament, but there he is. Mile after cussing mile he hangs there, almost certainly unable to stop quickly if you had to. This situation is called, Snort Pals. His engine snorts into your exhaust pipe, and vice versa. There is a cure for this.

CURE FOR THE SNORT PALS SYNDROME: get away from this risky situation. The AARP driving courses tell us to, "Simply slow down and let 'em pass." Ha! A true Snort Pal pays no attention to this hackneyed gimmick. His bumper keeps breathing engine-breath into your butt-end, as he is basically just not paying attention to his driving anyway. AARP's stale advice also makes for no fun. Rather, start by punching your cruise control up by one mile per hour. No more. He will unthinkingly adjust his speed up to yours. After 30 seconds, bump it up one more mile per hour. Do this again. And again. And again. And again, until you are now 11 mph faster than when you started, both you and your Snort Pal. Now you can reverse the sequence. Go back down one mph at a time, until you at last are going ten mph *slower* than when you started this dance. He may hang in there for a while in lockstep , uh, lock-bumper, but he eventually will gun his engine, pass you, and get back to actually paying attention to his driving. I have had only one Snort Pal not to go along with my excellent cure, behind me on a very straight two-lane road in Upstate New York. He must have been a foreigner, say, from Ohio.

Now, when you drive down multiple-lane roads and highways using good-driver techniques, you will very often attract Lane Pals. Lane Pals may look like ordinary traffic behavior, but there is a distinction. Unlike "normal," random traffic, a Lane Pal keeps his car beside and a little behind yours, for miles and miles, preferably in your blind spot. His car clearly must be in love at first sight with your car, because it's close enough to admire your bumpers.

CURE FOR THE LANE PALS SYNDROME: the "Snort Pals cure" won't work here, because the real problem is that the Lane Pal poses a worse danger to you. You hardly see him. So if you are not in a right lane, get there. Trust me, your Lane Pal will adjust his stupidity to match. Then quickly turn (right) into the Dough-Nut Shack and go order up a coffee to reward yourself. If no one was directly behind you before your fast right-turn caper, then do not signal the turn. The Lane Pal now faces a terrible new problem: you're gone. There would have been no way for him to make that same right turn without an embarrassing screeching of brakes, especially if you didn't signal. Of course, if there was a policeperson sitting there at the Dough-Nut Shack, you could have a different new problem. That last sentence has already earned some ugly email from various law-enforcement persons.

Some smart-aleck will no doubt point out that a Red Light Pal actually becomes the same thing as a Lane Pal when you are both stopped at the light. Yes, but you don't get that great cup of coffee you craved in the first place next to a Red Light Pal, pal. Don't be a Badger, Pal!

Stop and Smell the Electronic Roses

W hat's the difference between a person texting, and a cow chewing its cud? Answer: the intelligent look on the cow's face.

Whether 50,000 years ago, or fifty seconds ago, the human brain can only handle a few things all at once. The average, I understand, is only about five or six. I'm happy if I get three.

The sad news about these six things is that five of them will be focused on future events, thoughts or problems, and only one will be vaguely wandering on something right-now. The obvious exception is the juggler who manages two operating chain saws, two cleavers, a bowling pin, and a baby pineapple. All six juggler's thoughts are about the immediate juggled objects. If he doesn't, his new nickname will be *Lefty*.

The rest of us untalented persons fancy ourselves as juggling many, many important matters at the same time, all the time. We say that we are productive and distracted. We are half right; we are distracted jerks. Distraction is an excuse, though. *Attention* is the real problem. So assorted smart-alecks tell us to, "Stop and smell the roses."

This irritating bromide has been kicking around for at least a couple and one-half millennia. Why, Plato himself apparently "...decried the spread of writing," for example, because that *new* skill caused people to *think* less. Today most of us would say that writing time is just as good as straight noggin time. In fact, writing forces us to be 100% noggin anyway, with a little finger dexterity thrown in. Plato was kind of a prude, to boot.

History has just taken an historic leap, though.

We finally have come to the point in this modern time where many, many, many people *do* stop and smell the roses. It's called *texting* and *tweeting*. Let's go back to our person texting. Do this useful thought experiment. Walking down an urban street at morning rush hour, you hold a ten dollar bill up in front of you, about chest level. See how far you get before someone says, "Whaaathe..huh..." So many passers-by will be working at their texting machine or their tweeting machine, that they will pass the ten-buck miracle. Don't try this for real at evening rush hour, as more folks will have their mind on happy hour, and a handy sawbuck would sparkle like three medium diamonds in your fingers.

How is this all working out for us? We have a civilization raised on electronic fluff, quickly losing its personal civility. Civility demands personal attention, aimed toward each other.

Let's change that old faded bromide to, "You gotta' stop and toss that electronic *thingamajig* into the roses."

Rules for Misanthropes

Th 	ere are only three. First, though, take this story about the bed-n-breakfast.

Once upon an important time, sitting in a small conference room with several other business persons and generally minding my own bidness', I asked for suggestions about good local places I could go for a couple days to be by myself and finish writing an important project. This one. A place where I could spend time polishing up the final work, and doing so on my own cranky schedule, uninterrupted. All these good people, these friends, stumbled over each other touting *this* or *that* bed-n-breakfast. I erupted at the racket, "I am *not* going to a bed-n-breakfast. You see, I hate people!"

Laughter, laughter, laughter.

Actually, I put two ugly adjectives in front of that "bed-n-breakfast," though that's neither here nor there. For great productive and uninterrupted time, why on Jupiter would I want to *talk* to someone in the morning over coffee? The real way to have my coffee would be in a fat, heavy mug, which I would spill onto my papers, cuss, wipe it up, cuss some more, then top off the mug. Alone. God, that's fun! What a great way to lead into rule number one for misanthropes!

Rule Number One: Most of the time, prefer your own company.

Unless you don't. Like any self-respectable rule, you use it when it does some good. This one does you some good when *no one else's* thinking and judgment can possibly be better than yours. Look at it this way: no one else can digest your food for you either. Now, consider this next story.

"Did you find everything you wanted?" asks the gentle and helpful checkout-counter-person, as you drop umpteen unrelated items onto the checkout belt. You also see umpteen persons in the line behind you. Unloading all your stuff, extracting your wallet from your pants, and fishing out the cash or card to pay for the stuff is about all the things you can handle at the same moment.

"Now that you mention it," you say brightly, "I did mean to pick up a pack of Siamese cigars, fourteen paperweights, and a Galilean telescope (signed of course), and I am so glad you reminded me. Give me five or ten minutes, and I'll be back in a jiffy." Now, you neither want to ruin the clerk's morning, nor get pummeled by the umpteen line behind you, so this is all said with a light laugh. Look only at the clerk! The umpteen line behind you will get the joke if you do not make eye contact with it. They would rather kill you. Did I mention that this happened in a Dollar Store? So you see, you need this next, second rule for misanthropes to survive.

Rule Number 2: Treat most situations with an easy sense of humor.

(Remember, life is *not* short; it can be really long). In spite of the rough-sounding way I handled the first story, the fact that everyone around me knew I was kidding about "hating people" (mostly), it came out so stupidly that it *had* to be funny. It was. There are times when this rule doesn't fit, and this turns out to be a really, really serious problem, *to wit*:

Rule Number Three: Misanthropes have no obsession or compulsion to "be connected."

Cell phones are good, because you may need to call someone for help, order a pizza, or impress someone into thinking that you might actually be connected. Laptop computers are good for kind of the same reasons. Otherwise, why does any part of your intelligent-self need to have an electronic fishhook constantly into and from someone else? Why do you need a modern *here-I-am* medal?

Rule #3 bears an eerie likeness to rule number one. Take Twitter, for example. I personally plan to leave my first *twit*, once I learn how to do it, about how I pitched my cookies on an ocean trip decades ago, complete with colors, the part of the deck that got hit first, etc. I suppose I could get started by asking the nice lady texting next to me how she handles her twits. As for Facebook, one look at that monstrosity told me that I was seeing the very first serious industrial attempt at letting people digest other people's mental food for them. Maybe that would be a good first *twit*?

Fun with Math

P oor misanthrope. "He misses so many choices and possibilities in life."
Phoo!
By choosing to be around people, say, less than the *average* amount, of course the misanthrope will miss some chances to meet that "important person," or maybe to hear or see something that would have been worthwhile, or perhaps to savor some pleasant experience. Etcetera. In short, he will pass up by default a chance to learn something.

Let's flip this around a little. Let's think about the UN-misanthrope. Lets just say *anthrope*. It's shorter. Now, suppose our *anthrope*, eager to schmooze with bunches of assorted people, decides to see one person or group more per day than the average misanthrope does. This means that, over an average active person-meet life, the anthrope has 1 times 40 years times 365 days per year, which equals (in round numbers), *umm*, many thousand more encounters in a lifetime.

Bu-u-u-u-l-l-Lee!

Keep flipping it around. Just how much time do all these added encounters take, huh? Doing the round-numbers thing again, we get many thousands of encounters times, say, one and one-half hours per encounter, which equals (*umm*, divide by "x" and carry the "7," and adding gasoline for half those trips at two dollars and eighty-eight-point-nine cents a gallon....) about many more thousands of hours, and much gasoline phewing up the atmosphere. A rational anthrope will get tired just choking over these figures.

Point is, you end up with a large added effort to do all this encountering, so that even a half-rational anthrope has to wonder what value comes back for all the shoe- or ear- leather walked or listened-to. To be sure, he will certainly stumble into more opportunities than his "poor misanthrope" friend, because if you aren't "out there," "they" can't notice you. *("You can't make a hit unless you step up to bat." "You can't win the lottery unless you buy a ticket." "You can't catch any fish unless you buy a zillion dollars' worth of equipment, get up at dark-thirty in the morning, load up the old truck with 500 pounds of ice, spill coffee all over the front seat in a blind half-sleep, raw-haw-haw it up with your buddies about how much fun this is, forget to fill up the tank at two dollars and eighty-eight-point-nine cents a gallon ..." Oh, you get the idea).*

Think about this wisdom, though: "Even a blind 'possum can stumble over breakfast from time to time."

Not to belittle these stumbled-over contacts the anthrope finds himself cooing about. Some of these may be very good. Some of that blind 'possum's "found" breakfast may also actually be edible. Of course, a 'possum isn't all that picky. The thing is, the average misanthrope comes up with some sterling contacts also. Just not as many. His secret? He tends to think about what *fewer* contacts he will be making, most of those, to be sure, more enjoyable encounters than his anthrope buddy has.

Revisit those important Rules for Misanthropes. They don't say, "*always* prefer your own company." It isn't, "be humorous *all* the time." You can't get away with "*never* being connected." No, no, no. A true misanthrope chooses *when* to be alone with his own judgment, *how* to use humor in context sparingly, and *who* to be connected with—*whom*, just so we don't end that sentence where the preposition's at. This shows freedom at its best: the freedom for one to choose what to do next, and the freedom to fall on one's butt if things don't work out; since that last clause again tries to end a sentence on the wrong part of speech, we inserted this additional dependent clause in.

Other *phooey* goes to some other conventional wisdoms on this topic:

- "Be yourself." Great—then everybody can stay away from you right off the bat.
- "To thine own self be true." You are unlikely to call yourself out for lying to yourself.
- "If God had wanted me otherwise, He would have created me otherwise" (Johann von Goethe). Better luck next time around, Jo.
- "He who trims himself to suit everyone will soon whittle himself away" (Raymond Hull). There are a few of these "he-whos" to whom you might be tempted to hand your pocket knife.
- "The snow goose need not bathe to make itself white" (Lao Tzu). What?
- "The thoughtful soul to solitude retires" (Omar Khayyam). Damn, Omar, that's still pretty good!

Incidentally, why is our misanthrope constantly referred to as "he"? The grammar rule, might I remind you, is simply this: misanthropes are mostly thoughtful and cranky boys. Long ago a certain bus station bum added this great truth to my personal wisdom bag: "Girls is too smart for all that."

Once a Boy Always a Boy, and *Vice Versa*

Actually, "A rock, a boy, and a piece of glass." Wander through this image for a few moments. Put a boy in a bare, one-window room with a medium-size rock, and a fresh medium-size pane of glass on the floor.

+++++++

Come back one hour later, and the scene will always look the same when you open the door. In every case the boy will look at you and say, "Something happened!" or words to that effect. How the boy got there, though, will vary. Finding out how "something happened" will sparklingly predict the boy's future. Now, a scientist would tell us that "a large increase in local entropy *just happened*" (i.e., pieces of glass all over the floor). Philosophers just call this *preliminary cognitive boppage.*

Most boys will have simply picked up the rock and begun a light bopping cadence on the pane. *Tap, tap, tap. Tap, tap, tap, t-a-ap, tap, tap, tapatap-a-a-tap, t-a-a-a-a-ap-atatapa-taptaptapataptaptapataptapa*, and then "something happens."

Bless this boy, because he just instantly grasped the concept of "limits." If, after the sudden creation of pieces, the boy looks over his shoulder, he will surely be the solid kind of person who makes this country run, as he also understands the idea of "Uh, oh, my fault." If, however, he grins over the pieces and amuses himself about fitting the pieces together, he will become a star engineer. We need him, too. If he sweeps up the pieces and puts them in the trashcan, he will become a mediocre engineer, or at least a good family man, and we need oodles of these cats too. If he sweeps up the pieces and pitches them out the window to hide the evidence, he is headed for politics, and we could probably make do with fewer of these.

What if our boy instead stares at the glass pane for a while, deciding on the best deal to *happen* next? Many paths branch from this point. A large minority of these boys will stand back a distance from the pane and toss the rock in a casual direction toward the glass. Most of this grouping will be setting up a sort of game. For example, he might start at the opposite end of the room and take a pitch at the pane. If he misses, then he takes on step closer and tosses, repeating until *something happens*. Whatever form this game takes, you can see that you only get one "successful" try, so only one game version like this can be planned and played out. Thus, boys will learn valuable facts about *making choices.*

One special group bears extra watching. Every boy sees that the first rock will never break the pane into equal pieces. Most will toss or wield the rock once or twice, being satisfied that indeed the glass cracks loudly, and it's fun hearing that crash once or a couple times. What about those few who keep crashing and crashing the glass, making the shards smaller and more equal in size, down to crumbles?

Half of this weird group lines the pieces up and admires how they appear equal in size and uselessness. These good fellows have futures as politicians also, but of the extra wild and useless type. They likely will not serve many terms in their elected or appointed offices.

The other half of this group who like to equalize the pieces are stranger yet. They keep pounding and pounding until all the glass gets reduced to crumbs. They then carefully scrape the zillions of equal chips into nice geometric shapes. Maybe they form a circle, a triangle, or a square, or some creepy irregular thing. Not minding at all that all these sharp little pieces resist reforming, thus cutting his hand, he continues scraping until all the shards are in the perfect shape—his personal choice. This chap has *dictator* written all over him. He will need extra guidance for a few years.

Here's a better idea: a boy, an empty cardboard appliance carton, and a whole frozen chicken....

Stepping in Poop

Will this brilliant writer again give a great life analogy with a moral? Nope. Just facts.

Stepping in poop on a morning walk means *dog*. Statistics show that 98.1% of neighborhood poop is *canine*. The other 1.9% is divided among horse, cat, llama, Mars person, and kangaroo. There is no moral here, and utterly no reason for random doggie phoo lying around. Now a *work-around* for that unlucky stepper-inner person.

To clean off your shoe, at least the business parts, you have to use nature's scrub brush. I refer to that scraggly green strip that looks like grass, which struggles to grow between sidewalk and street. If you can start shoe-shuffling in front of pooch owner's house first, that would be ideal. Nevertheless, shuffle-scrub right away, although your new bad temper will kick-start you anyway.

Bystanders will empathize with your freestyle cussing. Experience shows that it takes about one mile of cuss-walking to take the edge off your anger, give or take a few hundred yards. Here is an excellent opportunity to experiment with new word combinations. The real challenge comes in making "clean" words sound like curse words by working them in with their shorter and less acceptable cousins, then spoken with feeling. Volume is an individual choice.

Ditto, in the winter season, except that snow and ice work the scrubbing part instead of grass. Just be careful not to slip and make a three- or four-point landing in the meantime. George Will, a famous news commentator and professional pundit, once said about the country's illegal drug problem, "Some things in the world just have to be called 'a mess.'" Well, Mr. Will, stepping in doggie mess ought to rise to the top of any list you can make up.

When Two Things Go Wrong

My father, a truly modest person and sometimes gifted genius on daily-living matters, had once offhandedly noted that when you have to fix something broken, and there is only *one* problem causing it, then you can usually solve it readily. When *two* problems are at the root—and the problems are not related—then it can be *hell* solving it. He didn't actually put it that way because he was indeed a modestly-spoken man. We were talking about fixing our cars at that time, and howling with laughter about it over chips and beer. The general principle, though, is still pure genius.

Take the car, for example. One very cold afternoon, say you park your out-of-date Ford Fairlane and head inside to your workplace. Earlier that morning you had noticed that the car started hard, and you meant to check out the electrical system, at least the big, accessible chunks. Your favorite aunt had lovingly given you that Fairlane, and you knew the wires, cables, hoses, caps, hangers, etc., were getting a bit elderly. Probably, the old car needed new just-about-everything in the next year.

Fast forward to getting out of work later that day. Much later, after it has been dark for a couple hours. Freezing wind howling at your muffless ears, you jump in the car and turn on the ignition key.

Cough, cough, die. Cough, cough, die. Damn!

Slowly getting out of the car, stomach feeling like you swallowed a small chunk of creosoted two-by-four, you raise the hood and routinely feel the electric cables for the loose *perp* causing the non-start. None. Still, maybe your healing touch magically connected something important, unseen. Try the key again anyway.

Cough, cough, die. Cough, cough, die, damn! Sigh.

Call your wife, who really doesn't mind rescuing you. The kids squeal delightedly about coming to rescue Daddy from Great Danger. You ought to look at that distributor cap, which means the poor wife has to turn the ignition key whilst you look for sparks around the cap. Sure enough, a faint, faint glow tells you that the *perp* has been cornered.

Tomorrow. Saturday. Yes, it is truly a new day dawning. Here you are, armed with a new distributor cap and a spray can of wire dryer stuff. Dirty Harry with earmuffs, you stride toward the Ford to face down the evil distributor cap.

New cap installed, electrical wires all sprayed, you get in and fire that baby up.

Cough, cough, die. Cough, cough, die, don't cuss in front of the family.

At this point, all armchair readers know that the car-repair "troubleshooting tree" should mentally kick in, because the engine still didn't. Ah, ha—freezing weather, old fuel lines, water in the gasoline (yes, a real problem back in "those days")—all these ugly causes pop up.

Back home for some jugs of very hot water, and an array of electrical-checking meters and tools to impress your wife, you return wearily chilled to the engine from *aitch-ee-double-ell*. This part of the story could be made long, but why bother. The hot water apparently melted the tiny, tiny plug of frozen water in the tiny, tiny tubing carrying gasoline to the carburetor.

Cough, cough, r-rr-rrr, cough, r-r-roooommmmm!

So here's the important point in this ridiculous story: there truly were two things wrong with the old Ford, one electrical, one fuel-line, neither of which were related, but both of which cursed you at the same moment. Simultaneously, together, in unison, at the same time. Both prevented the car from starting.

This Two-Things-Wrong happens in other areas as well. Medically, how many allergy sufferers have come down with a cold on the exact initial first day when the lilac blossoms pop outside the back door? Real allergy pros can tell the difference after a short time. What about that first day in the season, though? *Hell's bells*, it just isn't fair, even if this is not the most fatal problem to wake up with!

Now, how does one deal with those relatively rare Two Things Wrong events? Because of their rarity, the average Jake immediately heads to Despair Village. Misanthropes belonging to the more cynical fringe will be in much better shape mentally, because they *know* they have been targeted by the Fates for a major Two-fer. All misanthropes, however, will then instinctively do the most important act: think. We think about whether the problem situation *tastes* like a Two Things Wrong*er*.

Rare or not, these *Two-fer* events show up often enough in life to need some illustration. Here are three examples.

Problem: "The Political Slum Dunk." First thing to go wrong: you listened to the political talk from the assortment of candidates. Second thing to go wrong: you voted for the boob. Or the pretty face. Or both. Dumb.

Problem: "The Birthday Bollix." First thing to go wrong: you buy flowers, which wilt in your car trunk.

Second thing to go wrong: you are a day late. See, because you cheapskated out on calendars two years ago and accepted two free identical calendars mailed to you by the Llama Coiffeurs Galactic Institute, you pulled a massive boner. Yes, you boob, you get a day behind that way; two, if it's a leap year. You inconsiderate boob. You cheap, inconsiderate, dog-house boob. Now, you could have insured yourself against this lapse: get a bracelet instead of flowers. Forgiveness gets back quicker from jewelry than from flowers of mulch quality. Oh, get flowers too, but at least generate enough energy to bring them into the basement overnight. Also, do not forget to water them, you inconsiderate, cheapskate, calendar-dummy boob.

Problem: "The Breast Exam Debacle." For the target population of good people, the first thing to go wrong: you forget the set up an appointment. Second thing to go wrong: you don't wanna' go. "Boob" ain't going to be used here, because it ain't funny.

Green

K ermit was really only partly right about "being hard to be green." This truth is sometimes false. Take one of these three *green* things, for example: a zillionaire with lots of greenbacks, a vine-hugger, or a frog. Only one of those is actually easy.

Zillionaire-tude has to be difficult because you have to make *one* million greenbacks before graduating to *many* zillions. I, personally, tell everyone that I am working on my second million. See, the first million didn't work out, so I skipped it and moved briskly along to the second. What the average Brian doesn't realize is that it really *isn't* easier to make the *nth* million dollars than the first one.

Yes, a million in First National Cheater Bank will earn interest without your lifting a finger. The amount of interest you get, however, won't be much greater than lifting a *motionless* finger. At the current generous rate of nearly zero percent, your grandchild could harvest your sixty-five bucks in built-up interest and really whoop it up. To be fair, this calculation is wrong. He or she would only collect about 45 bucks' interest, you having pre-harvested a couple Franklins in principal for pizzas along the way, just to blunt the pain of doing all this math.

Calculating interest can be boring. The next paragraph will talk about interest, but it will not be boring. It will also last only one paragraph. Some time in the vague future, hopefully before all you readers die, when bank interest rates yield 3-1/2 percent again, your bank account would double in about twenty years.

Now, recall the fable of the sultan's vizier who, when asked what reward he wished for his long and valuable service, said he wanted only to fill a common checkerboard with grains of wheat. He asked for only one grain on the first square, two grains on the second square, four grains on the third square, and so on, doubling each time. Each next square doubled the vizier's money (wheat). It turns out that by merely the 25th square, the vizier becomes unbearably wealthy, at least in wheat futures. "The power of doubling"! All right, so what? Well, swapping this parable into your 3-1/2 percent interest rate situation, you too double your money after each "square," but the bad news is that your life only lasts four more squares, tops. Bank interest is really a hard way to become a green zillionaire.

Anyway, the already-zillionaires will tell you that as your stash mounts, people will notice that. Smart people notice that. Smart, competitive people notice that. These kinds of smart people are very good at copying what you do and horning in on your territory. Since most of these will actually be smarter than you, they will invent new ways to copy what you do *before* you think about it. Green by zillionairing, if you so choose, will indeed turn out to be very hard.

What a silly thing to call green environmentalists: "Vine huggers!" No one hugs vines! People *do* hug boulders and barrel cacti, though. In fact, if you want to raise big bucks for your environmental club, one possible cactus recipe suggestion, sold from a street hotdog vendor's wagon, is "saguaro-on-a-stick." The needles may be a little tricky to eat around, but what the heck? Burros have learned to eat cactus fruits with those selfsame spines, and most burros seem healthy.

Greening by environmental work & stuff looks easy in the beginning, but just hold your zebras here. Let's say, for example, that you will only order pizza takeout from establishments that use cartons made exclusively from recycled materials. Have you ever thought about—no, researched—*what* exact materials are being recycled? The gray mass of bulky stuff comprising the recycled carton may be effective, but toxic substances may be in the mix, such as old tires, leftover food items, or paperback books published by essay writers.

Equally bad, those recycled substances could be "clean," but fall apart after a short ride. This debacle normally happens after buying a super-loaded-meats pizza with extra whole tomato slices, and generally onto slacks with a light-colored material. There's nothing like the good-old-fashioned standard nontoxic, non-natural material carton that keeps your light-colored slacks out of trouble.

And what is it with these plastic bags? Plastic bags actually got evolved by unemployed geniuses who did not like the fact that paper shopping bags came from trees. Actually, these get shipped in by night from Zimbabwe. Anyway, these good green folks insisted on switching to polyethylene bags, because paper bags came from trees, which had to be cut down, which means they disappeared, which means until the five saplings planted to replace each old one grew up.

Meanwhile, the polyethylene bags (with those handle-like strappy things which cut the palms of your hand when loaded with fourteen pounds of goodies) get thrown away into the trash, which means they go into a landfill, where they last for five trillion years. The green answer: manufacture the bags to be more "biodegradable," which means load up the plastic formula with starches, which means they break in seven minutes when loaded with more than one-half pound of leftover tomato sauce, halfway to the big garbage can outside, which means you have to first put the biodegradable bag into a handy *paper* bag. Gads, do you see how confusingly hard it is to be an environmental-green?

By now it won't take much to convince even Socrates that, by far, the easiest of these three green things to be is a frog. For a bonus, as a green frog you could have a rich prince or princess stumble along and give you a big hug & kiss. Think about it, but don't count on it.

Carbon Footprints

S o, how big is your carbon footprint? Do you even know what that means? Does that include all the carbon atoms which you, you filthy Homo sapiens *sapiens*, exhale into the atmosphere with each out-breath? If so, then everyone's carbon footprint would come out pretty much the same, depending only on how many years one lived. But no! This extremely large amount of exhaled carbon—carbon dioxide— does not count these days into the Personal Official Carbon Footprint.

These are the kind of things that officially count, we suppose from the Official Carbon Footprint Headquarters (OCFH): driving vehicles, heating and cooling buildings, and making stuff. The listed "stuff" includes paper, plastics, candy wrappers, glass, cans, computers, carpet, tires, lumber, paved roads, letters and packages, beer cans, water bottles, wasted water, light bulb burning, dead trees and foreign food. Hmmm. Noticeably missing from this list would be concrete making and pouring, charcoal grilling and beer itself.

In fact, all of these listed items only come from things that are manufactured or farmed. In *further* fact, the accused carbon *perp* making all these nasty clomping footprints sounds like that same *carbon-dioxide* word. Heavens, this is the same stuff we just found out we exhaled! *Methane* doesn't count, although this is a far worse greenhouse gas, and comes from natural gas wells and other dead or belching fauna.

So let us not quibble with the OCFH. Let the scepter of guilt fall squarely on non-breath carbon dioxide. Go back to the listing of carbon footprint *perps*. "Driving around," and other assorted uses of internal combustion machinery (gas vehicles) comprise the fattest carbon feet. Besides Homo sapiens *sapiens* exhaling, of course. The next biggest grouping is building heating and cooling. The point of this technical topic should now begin to be clear. Driving to work at a climate-comfortable workplace, and then returning to a climate-comfortable living place has created a world of hard-working, but comfortable-living troglodytes, carbon clomping all over the place.

Before stating the obvious answer to reducing the world-people's average footprint, we add one more concept: the Carbon Exchange. Here is how such an exchange works at a high level. People who make lots of carbon footprint can exchange for carbon credits, "attaboys," from people who make very small footprints. Carbon slobs pay these "carbon anorexics" for their credits. The slobs get to feel better, and the small-carbon-makers get cash.

Now do you see the obvious solution to the rampant carbon size-24 ecological shoe prints? Simple: quit your job, and live in a low heat & cool apartment. You won't drive anywhere, and you won't need a thermostat in your living space. You will have to, of course, sell or switch wherever you live for a small center-located apartment in a huge rental complex, sometimes called a "workers' paradise." How can you do this? Who pays for your eats and beer? Now comes the truly brilliant part.

The Authority for Carbon Exchange (ACE) makes all this happen, don't you see? As a non-employed, no-thermostat-twiddling person, you have almost no visible carbon footprint. You create out of thin, non-polluted air carbon credits which you can now sell. You are entitled to use the ACE to rip oodles of cash from the fraction of slobs who still choose to stomp out huge carbon footprints.

And who might these latter shameful persons be? Why, the remaining employed persons who drive to work and have to live in the top, outside wall, or bottom units in your workers' paradise. These are the dwellers who must use their thermostats to keep their units from frying or freezing, and to keep yours at even temperature. Location, location, location!

That third category of big-footprint makers, roughly consisting of manufactured or farmed things, matters much less. Our heroic, virtuous souls who do not work, drive, or who do not hike thermostats will not be able to buy large amounts of these goodies in any case. Such would require taking so much cash from those mean, inconsiderate working stiffs that they would get really mad. Low-carbon saints probably do not need that many worldly goods anyway. Since they do not drive, they also take no trips or vacations.

One sad downside to this otherwise flawless plan will be the shortened life expectancies of the small-carbon-footed population. No driving, no stimulating job, no trips, no vacations, no thermostat fiddling, fewer than average goodies to play around with, all contribute to a grayer lifestyle. More meals will feature oatmeal, kidney beans, and cabbage. Life expectancies, clearly, will end up a little under the general population average. Whether from the drab diet while living or the inevitable decay after dying, these persons will necessarily exude much methane, one way or another. We have proved earlier, though, that methane doesn't count. Let this Great Plan now move forward.

The Heavy Carbon Foot Stomps Again

So many cranky emails poured in after a trial run of "Carbon Footprint," that I must publish a further clarification. "Further clarifications" work poorly for politicians, but better for us writers. Noting that the emails fell into two angry groups, I tackled each in turn. Here is a sample of incoming emails with helpful input about matters I left out, mostly caused by my stupidity. My answers or thoughts are in set in braces { }:

"What would be the carbon footprint of a Prius whose battery burned the car to the ground, leaving a crispy black Prius-shaped shadowy scum in the driveway?" {Hard to calculate.}

"Why not just say that the Authority for Carbon Exchange (ACE) simply trades your trash on the way in the door, for a kick in the butt on the way out the door?" {Too crude.}

"Doesn't a business using old, gas-eating pickup trucks to deliver solar panels to government buildings have a bad carbon footprint?" {Probably not; they get *good-guy credits.*}

"Aren't carbon credits exactly like Medieval 'indulgences'?" {Certainly not! No actual coins change hands today, at least not over the counter, and not bulky old coins either.}

The second angry group of emails, also helpful, had to do with various interesting facts and thoughts I left out, mostly caused by my stupidity. Here is a sample from this lively group:

"You didn't give credit to the original lowest-carbon-footprint organization in history—the Boy

Scouts." {Yep. Author's error. Scouts' get major credit, and not of the carbon-credit type.}

"How could you fail to tell readers how easy it is to count your carbon footprint? I mean, there are numerous websites that do this." {Fair enough, though it might be prudent to do two of these: one by, say, the Sierra Club and the other by the Coal Miners and Burners Society. Average the two for meaningful results.}

"Are you implying that the good low-carbon citizenry are dawdling, uninspired, unadventurous, low-energy, denizens? You are truly a mouth-breathing, insulting, uninspiring clod yourself, you pontificating misanthropic old poop!" {Too crude.}

"Hey, Misanthrope. Check your carbon?" {Nope.}

Enough time on personal problems, all of which eventually get sorted out. The time has come for a truly elegant solution to the carbon-footprinting problem. Scientists love *elegant solutions* to scientific problems, because it's easier to create a viral podcast when you say you have found one. They get rave popular reviews, before the experiment checking prudes and mathematicians show up. *Rare back*, roll up your sleeves, and ready your brain now for this *elegant solution*:

Gradually substitute your carbon body parts with silicon-based parts!

Oodles of scientific papers have been written about life based on silicon, as the silicon atom and the carbon atom lie in the same chemical "family," making for remarkably parallel chemistry in many cases. The trouble is, experiments are sorely needed to test these scads of theories on actual fauna. *You* can become the experimental hero. Being the first person to do so will assure you of millions in research grants. Money will pour in by the lake full. Famous Nobel personages will cluster around your house like paparazzi on pizza, and your exchequer will overflow.

The aim of these bold experiments: you will no longer exhale carbon dioxide. You will instead breathe out *silicon dioxide*—sand. Think of it. The largest, but now uncounted amount of carbon dioxide released to the air comes from animals exhaling. In the future, exhaling counts as *extra credit*! Now the carbon dioxide disappears from the atmosphere, making up for all that driving, building, heating & cooling, etc., we Homo sapiens *sapiens* do otherwise.

Think also about the personal benefits of your complete body silicon changeover. After a while, you would never have to spend time and money going to the beach. You simply exhale your own, right outside your house. The neighborhood cats will be overjoyed, to boot. Getting sand in your shoes and your hair now becomes a non-problem. Also, you could change your nickname to a cool "Sandy," which will fit both genders.

On the minus side, you do not want friends slapping you on the back with congratulations, as you might shatter. You will be forbidden access to golf courses because they do not want customers exhaling more sand traps. Also, your food intake will have to change. Now that carbohydrates and other carbon-based macronutrients are out, you will have to find other products to satisfy your silicon-based hunger. Maybe this will not be so difficult. We would likely turn around an old expression, happier this time, "Eat dirt, and *live!*"

"Bueller.... Bueller....?"

R ecognizez-vous the phrase? Of course you do! Everyone recognizes this piece from the classic movie "Ferris Bueller's Day Off." Everyone will also remember the deadpan face of Ben Stein, the teacher who was mumbling the phrase, even if they do not recall his name.

Mister Doctor Ben Stein has the good fortune to have loaded his life with being not only actor (infrequent), but also a screenwriter, lawyer, professor, author, economist, consultant, and TV talking head (frequent). In later years, he has been talking and writing about how enormously grateful he is for his good fortune and full life.

Readers may place Ben Stein's face as a TV essayist on Sunday Morning (CBS). If so, then one might think from his monologues that this man has a dry, but kindly sense of humor. True.

This unusual gent sports an unusual mix of viewpoints, even economic ones. Anyway, what on earth gives an economist the right to prattle on about economics, of all things? This task traditionally gets learned discussion by average persons-on-the-street, as everyone knows. Darn it that's our job! Allowing us that tradition, then, Mr. Stein talks about other matters, such as living a worthwhile life. Thankfully, the man makes much more common sense than other mouthy you-are-so-great promoters these days. *Economics* as a topic, on the other hand, makes so much less sense, even with a large mug of coffee.

Recently Mr. Stein has published on an enormous reach of topics—advice—about the value of being a straightforward, thoroughly honest person of good will.

All the time, always. Topics range from marriage ("A Big, Big Deal") to tipping ("Tipping"!).

Personal financial advice coming from this man makes more sense in a shorter space than from just about anyone else. Always, always, he leans hard on the importance of personal character and integrity. A short piece titled "I Am Just Like You, Only I Am Me" should rank as the finest and clearest essay on personal "balance" I have ever read, and found on page 93 of <u>What Would Ben Stein Do?</u> (John Wiley & Sons, Inc.). Do find a copy and read it.

Want to be rich? Get married and stay married to the same person. After your laughter peters out, do the math, both you and your wallet. Spouse too, if you're smart. You keep more of your wealth that way, not to mention the infinite value of keeping your life intact.

Barometer Contest

A priest, a rabbi, and a nuclear engineer walk into a bar, and…….. no, no, no! Never start out with such prejudice—by making persons of the cloth associate with an engineer! Here's a better P.C. way to begin-again-Finnegan. Something like this could happen to you one day, so pay attention.

Your local radio station, WDUM, sponsors this Science Day contest that will award five hundred dollars for the first person to show the calculation of the height of that big four-story city office building downtown, using a barometer and a thermometer. No using architectural records and no asking any of the city council-persons. Here is how you can dazzle the contest judges, and show how science stumbles happily into common-sense daily life. You are going to demonstrate not only *three* amazing ways to come up with the right answer, but also show that all three answers match. Genius!

Grab a ball of string, and the barometer and thermometer which the contest committee gives you and get started with the first clever method of determining the building height:

Method #1: the *Proportional Shadows Proposition*. We know you will get a sunny day for the contest because WDUM always opens the day's programming by saying so. Start by holding the barometer on the ground straight up to get its maximum shadow length. Measure the barometer's shadow. Also measure the length of the barometer itself. You can use your known body-parts dimensions such as knuckle length, arm length, hand span, etc. Write both dimensions down.

Quickly walk over to the building and measure its shadow length. Pace it off, and that will be close enough. You now have all the numbers you need! Since you know the building stands dead straight up, and you held the barometer straight up, your plane geometry teacher would tell you that you have two "proportional right angles." That's right! The relationship of the building's height to its shadow length is the same as the barometer's shorter length is to its smaller shadow. Your simple non-math-majors math here: multiply the length of the building shadow times the barometer length, then divide by the barometer shadow's length. The math is so simple, you can scrawl out the answer in the dirt. Voila! Q.E.D.!

Important process note: measure both shadows at almost the same time, because the sun moves and shadows change. Well, it's really the earth that turns.... If you dare take a siesta between measurements, then you will be very wrong and foolish, you lazy, lumbering lout. You will want to complete #1 promptly and move along to:

Method #2: the *Pendulum Clock Caper*. Clamber up the building stairwell to the roof. Don't walk, but clamber briskly for style points.

- Tie a long string to the barometer and gently lower toward the ground.
- About three-quarters down, start swinging the strung barometer slowly left & right to make a pendulum. Do not smash the barometer into the side of the building, and do not fall off the building in your excitement over this brilliant experiment.

- Gently lower the whole *shebang* until it almost touches the ground, and still swinging gently like a pendulum.
- Now time the pendulum swing from fully left to fully right. You can do the timing with your own pulse for added showoff points.
- Jot down the time when the barometer stops swinging left, until it stops swinging right. Check your work three times.

The math is a bit more involved here, so will have to be researched before the day of the contest. Knowing the pendulum swing time will get you the building height. [Trick, or extra-credit question: the thermometer weighs twice what the barometer weighs. If you use the thermometer instead of the barometer, will this change the result? If you didn't know that the correct answer is "no," or if you even doubt that, then this whole piece won't make sense to you.]

Important process note: if you do fall off the top of the building, you cannot finish method #2. You would be able to move to method #3, ahead of time, though:

Method #3: the *Fall Guy Technique*. If you are still standing on top of the building, then

- Drop the barometer and time its fall to the ground. Your pulse will work splendidly here also.
- The time of the fall will give you the exact building height (gravity is cruel, but it's the law). As with Method #2, the mathematics will be omitted here because the sight of that "per second squared" in the formula will reduce the number of people buying this book. Not good.

- Check your work by next dropping and timing the thermometer. (Same trick question and same trick answer as #2 above.)

Important process note: if you fell off the building during Method #2, then you likely have screwed up royally. UNLESS ... you had the presence of mind to time your fall, in which case you will finish Method #3 way ahead of time. You will be unable to check your work, so stay conscious long enough after you hit the dirt to scrawl down your fall time. In the dirt. You will have to figure in a higher heart rate than normal, of course.

There you have it! You have measured the height of the building with a barometer and a thermometer using three creative and brilliant ways, complete with cross-checked answers. Five fabulous hundred bucks, here you come!

****

A few hours later, though, the judges surprisingly announced another winner, some smart-aleck kid. They say he came up with strange methods, something everyone's buzzing about like, "barometric pressure-temperature gradients." Maybe they said, "borrowed grated prosciutto tapas," or something like that.

The kid clearly had beginner's luck, or he knows the mayor. You can't win with good fortune or outright rampant favoritism working for the other side.

One of Those Holiday Letters

Dear Friends&Others,

We knew it had been a good year when Rod's parole officer sent us a fruitcake last week. The dear man called a couple days later and said, "I thought you might like something with nuts in it around the house." Or maybe he said, "Is that Nut still around the house?" We forget which. Anyway, that wonderful gentleman promised to come over sometime this year and take Rod's ankle bracelet off. They're running short at State, and Rod, being his usual generous self, insisted that we "render back to Caesar what Caesar gave, etc., etc."

Sweet Letitia's occipital lobotomy went well. She moves around the house with her accustomed and well-known grace, practicing over and over her speech for the holiday party her former employer is giving next month. Although unasked to give any speech, you know Letitia! She believes they will be so delighted to hear about all the many things they could do to "clean up their act" around the office—professionals always like it when you point out the shortcomings of their business, so they can improve. And we know they will be so pleased to hear her list of just how some of the personalities there are hurting the business, too. We have just heard, though, that the party may be cancelled because of impending bad weather. Can you imagine, three weeks in advance. Those people at her old office are so SMART, aren't they!

Unfortunately, the frost killed off the *cannabis* bushes we were so carefully tending in the back yard. Damn. A whole winter's supply down the drain! Now we'll have to buy the stuff from friends or relatives.

Some neighbors have hinted that someone close by us called the cops, but you know, we DON'T live in that sort of neighborhood. Since we believe that adversity builds strength, we think this is a wonderful opportunity to expand. For instance, there are probably dozens of other marvelous and ~~hallucinogenic~~ healthful herbals which we could grow next year to fill new and unexpected gaps. If only we can get through the winter .....

Which brings up another important topic. Since we hear all of you are doing so extraordinarily well, we believe with all our wrenching hearts that you will be able to assist us in our time of GREAT TRANSITION. Peace be with you, and all the love and affection of you lovable friends&others, [our convenient website at *www.friends&others.~~com~~ zwe*, e-commerce-ready]

A parting note to our friends: people in the know no longer use the word "weed" for a green, dried leafy product consumed by smoking. The correct term these days is "snoggers."

Love,

Rod and Letitia

Forgetting Stuff

L ike anything else in the universe, you can lump all "forgotten stuff" into one of three categories:

Number One: Forgetting birthdays.
Number Two: Forgetting car keys.
Number Three: Forgetting that cup of coffee you stashed in the 'fridge.

Yes, *everything* in the entire set of "forgotten stuff" can be made to fit into one of these three groups. Some examples may take a bit more pounding than others to fit, of course. People have come up to me excitedly waving their arms around with silly questions such as, "Well, in what group would you put that chunk of broken concrete you intended to use as a doorstop?" Well, but who cares? If pressed, it can be easily shown that the cement *objet d'art* belongs squarely in—no, not with the car keys—the *coffee in the 'fridge* group. As I said, who cares!

For those puzzled about how these groups cover the universe, sit back for a relaxed tour. First, *forgotten birthdays* cover all the events, persons, or icons which needed your honorable mention at, or by, a certain date or time, or both. Some are serious; most are not. The test is this: will you "hear about it later"? Simple.

For forgotten *persons*, depending on the seriousness about "hearing about it later," an apology, perhaps some flowers or a token, and some humorous phrase will serve you well. For certain age groups, the outburst, "Just wait 'til you're 94 years old!" settles things down nicely. If you are below that age range, then say, "Well, that's democracy for you!" or maybe,

"Well, one thing at a time." For some reason, all of these work. Who knows!

Forgotten *events*, though, present no one to talk to directly. You may have some extra smoothing over to do. Ask yourself if your forgetfulness has just cost you a check or a wad of cash, a loss to someone else, or a hot date. For these, you must work even more smoothly. In most cases, though, F.I.D.O.: Forget It and Drive On. There will be larger and more spectacular chances to forget stuff later along.

We shall not dwell on forgotten *icons*. These cannot make you "hear about it later." These cannot even talk. A classical burnt offering will do, using an inexpensive, but traditional beast.

The *car keys*' grouping includes most tangible items. These forgotten items tend to be serious because they encourage you to cuss, and little cussing events may add up by the thousands, shaving hours off your life. In a few cases, this might mean *saving* a few hours off your life. Although possibly not soothing, the following Truth applies: There are 16 logical places where any object can be found. Further, just like Henny Youngman said, "Everybody has to be somewhere," then every *object* has to be somewhere. Unless someone has pitched it into the garbage disposal (rest in pieces—F.I.D.O.). Assume the best, though, and move along with this example: car keys.

Car keys could be in one of these 16 logical places:

1—on the hook where they "should be"
2—in the front door
3—in the side door
4—in your pants pocket
5—in your pants *other* pocket

6—on the kitchen counter
7—on the workbench
8—on the stairs, on the way up (down)
9—in the driveway
10—in today's coat pocket
11—in yesterday's coat pocket
12—in the lock that gets unlocked by one of the other keys on the chain
13—balled up with an undershirt in the hamper; this is embarrassing, but logical
14—under a cushion on the sofa
15—on the closet floor, under the coat part
16—(add your own personal experience, *logical*)

The car keys will *not* be in the garbage disposal, nor will they be at another address if your car is in the driveway—both are clearly *not* logical places. As for your dog....

Since repeating this drill with other personal items will only make readers madder, we will switch to another kind of example: where do you find chocolate syrup in the store? Well,

1—with the milks?
2—with the other dairy products, inconveniently located in a different place?
3—with the breakfast cereals?
4—with the Ovaltine®?
5—with the ice cream?
6—in a display shelf at the end of the bread row?
7—in a display shelf at the end of a random row?
8—on one of those annoying grocery-store rolling "islands" where they hang bananas?
9—with the candy?

10—with the syrups and stuff?
11—in the baking supplies and raw materials aisle?

That's eleven, and the list could extend to more than sixteen logical places if you include C-stores, but the principle is the same. When you can't find, or have forgotten where something sits, you have a choice: cuss and stamp a hole in the floor, or think. Or do both to clear your head.

Ah, yes, the *coffee in the 'fridge* group. This group includes the most useless, but most interesting examples. It is also huge. It dwarfs the other two. Almost no one thinks about this correctly, however. Since the human brain cannot focus on more than a handful of things going on at one time, the zillions of stimuli that assault the senses every second mostly have to be ignored. Your brain will anyway. At any one instant, your poor battered attention span has to deal with everything from butterflies to submarine sandwiches, to falling bowling balls. You can see that lots of odd, ignored items such as underwear, pencils, and coffee cups are good candidates for putting in some other ignored place. This place could easily be the refrigerator.

Twenty-dollar bills never fall into this last category. There is a lesson here somewhere.

A Euthanasia for All Seasons

F ear not: there will be only one graph in this entire book. It's going to show up right here. Although there are no Rules for Geezers (as for misanthropes), we do note some important *guidelines* making the rounds these days. This picture-graph below is worth a thousand rules. We will not go into detail about who wrote what, etc., but this graph appeared in the January 31, 2009, online issue of The Lancet magazine, and goes by the label "Complete Lives Theory" or "Useful Lives Theory." Friendly sounding tags, 'eh?

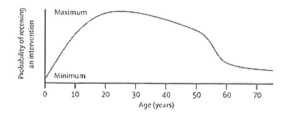

There are too many stuffy words on this vague picture, so let us shorten what the thing truly says. Persons younger than a certain age, AND older than a certain age are less valuable to society than the persons in the middle (where the graph bumps upward). Whatever *less-* and *more-valuable* mean. Whatever *society* means. Very young people have not had enough investment in education yet, the thinking goes, and older people have had enough life already. Whatever *enough* means. So if your age lies at either the right or left ends of the graph, then you pretty much don't count. Not much medical help coming your way!

All right, this graph will have to show up a few more times to prove the next points, but it is the same graph, so please go along with the program a painless hair longer. Note below the graph version which the younger geniuses in our government would like to use:

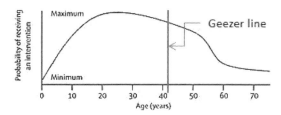

Going with this picture means that a whole bunch of people get lopped off the *aged* end into the "don't count" bucket. Old bucket persons, of course, are easier and cheaper to keep. Whatever *keep* means. *"To the buckets, you fellow geezers, this time for keeps!"*

Now compare this different picture—same graph, but different idea where to place the Geezer Demarcation Line. Using this new and more intelligent location most definitely allows for a fuller development of a complete life, a useful life. Certainly it gives a little more time for us older coots:

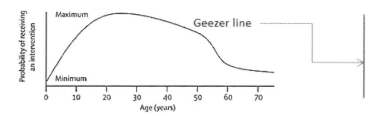

We citizens could go back and forth over *who* is wielding the line-demarker chalk today, and we would still not end this lively debate. Just when we thought we were stuck, though, a clever idea arose from the technical community. When ideas *arise from the technical community*, the world goes "ooooo, aaaaaaah!" Consider what happens when you invert the Complete Lives Theory chart (in technical words, "You flip the graph over."):

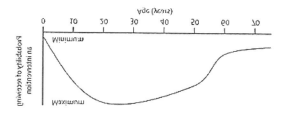

Now the graph won't be humped-up in the middle, but rather will look like a bowl with the sides dished up. Wow! Persons of toddler age and geezer age now become the most *important* groups to society!

Alas, we cannot have this version either because the good folks in the middle pay most of the bills, mainly because there are so gosh darn many of them. To settle all this in a person-friendly way, with malice toward none, let us make the graph a mere straight line across:

No important bulges stick up in the middle or either end of this picture. Now, *everybody* is good! We can call this the Flat Line Theory.

Maybe this doesn't sound so friendly either.

No more graphs! Poppy promises, for real. Maybe some math, but really easy stuff to make ridiculous philosophical points....

Envy, the Other Movie

Envy: I command you to spend not a minute more of your life on it. Yeah, yeah, I know. Moses already beat me to that envy commandment stuff by several millennia or so, but by the time his motley mob got far enough along enough to deserve all of those Commandments, they weren't paying much attention anyway. Also, they couldn't read. It was not helpful that they made up for it with some occasional heavy drinking. Besides, it apparently was written in Ancient Hebrew, and no one thought to pack a translating dictionary during the flight from Egypt. Not a dictionary donkey was to be found in the flight parade.

Envy is one of those Commandments that are not illegal, at least in common-law systems, but it certainly can ruin a good day. Doctors, Dale Carnegie, and psychologists also say it ruins good vascular and nerve systems, what with dumping bad biochemical molecules into the bloodstream, and so forth. The real problem with envy is that it isn't *real*. Envy is less tangible than say, email, which only consists of electrons in empty space. Envy hasn't even got the electrons, unless you stretch the science past breaking.

There is a recent movie by this name starring Ben Stiller and Jack Black, directed by Barry Levinson. The story has to do with a friendship being ruined because of the commercial success of one of the two friends. It seems one of them invented a product to make dog poop disappear. No doubt a valuable idea—*poop to poof*. The other friend gets envious of his pal's success, and one bad movie thing leads to another.

Here's the plot of "Envy, the Other Movie." From nowhere comes this harmless looking new hire to work with the Main Hero in a high-tech firm (what other kind?). Little by little, said new hire begins showing his great Omen-like evil competence, slowly putting the Hero into the new man's poisonous shadow. The new guy turns more and more sinister, becoming a sort of commercial antichrist, who threatens to absorb and conquer not only the company, but its entire Dow Jones industrial sector. Hardly anyone recognizes the expanding business evil except—of course—our Hero.

Now the movie Hero, himself a super-talented supercomputer programmer and analyst—of course—snapping out of his fog at last, captures his own burning red and green envy, which has almost overwhelmed him, and downloads this raw emotion into a new organic stealth app that he just concocted. Disguising this app as a quarterly financial update attachment onto a harmless looking email to the evil guy, he forwards this hot app. When the email and attachment get opened, POOF! The bad guy becomes immediately infected by massive envy, blinding him into committing blunders daily, just like a regular employee.

The movie ends with a large company awards ceremony, and then everyone walks off the set hand in hand. Wouldn't that be jes' *won'naful*? Add some action, a few Kazakh spies, a bunch of sex, some unintelligible dialog, Alec Guinness's ghost, and you have a film worthy enough to at least air on SyFy channel.

Can't happen to you in real life exactly that way, you say? But what if you wrote up a long and complete description of some poisonous personal envy of your own, though, then encrypted it into a format that *nobody* could open, then you are 90% there. When sent, your intended targets couldn't open the attachment, especially if password-protected, and you *don't want* them to open it anyway. They do not "get infected," but the whole drill would be enormously good for you as you feel the envy molecules slowly evaporate into electrons.

Do try this at home.

See? You can talk about nature MUCH more factually—more interestingly, anyway—if you aren't limited by old prejudices. Now, on to the crucial and clever talk about words & language….

THE NATURE OF WORDS

Genre

People incorrectly use this pesky word to mean a type of literary or artistic grouping. The correct modern meaning is to illustrate what a complete snob you are about literary or artistic matters while standing around with other like persons at a group mixer with a cup of coffee. "Fair trade," of course.

Almost no one knows that *genre* goes way, way back to the Battle of Genre in late Roman times. Little detail has escaped to this day, but we assume the intended battle took place between the Frenches and the Latins. Of this, we are certain because to this day standard English dictionaries give the word origin of *genre* as either Old French (OFr.) or Latin (Lat.). Everybody knows that anything Latin is already old, so the dictionary rarely says "OLat."

We do not know the strength of either armed force, nor do we know much about the weapons used. Scholars have, however, ruled out gunpowder and llamas. The Frenches had not invented a dependable one-syllable name for "match" yet, and the Latins couldn't figure out how to say that llama double "L."

One fact is certain, however. The actual battle was never fought. Nope! You see, it turns out that there were two *Genres* in western Europe at the time, and the generals got thoroughly confused about where to attack. This is also the origin of the phrase spoken by English majors at literary or artistic mixers, "To which genre are you referring to?"

Since both cultures prided themselves on initiative and audacity in the attack, we believe that the Latins immediately headed up north to Frenchia, and the Frenches headed south to Latinia. Since both societies were also ardent fair-traders, each army marched by different expensive routes but ended up with nothing at the other end.

Proof of this history clearly shows up today in the region of Turin in Italy, and in southeastern France. One only has to get a travel agent to book a trip to Via Genre, 12036 Revello CN, Italy. Then the following week to Genre Humain, 32 Rue République, 69002 Lyon, France.

Be sure to ask a local travel guide when you get there to tell you the full, exciting details about the Battle of Genre. Perhaps you shouldn't. Unless you display a generous gratuity, in which case you will get a two and one-half hour talk, with maps.

Proverbs, Deadly Proverbs

"Good to begin well, better to end well."
"A thing begun is half done."

P roverbs can make sense when taken one at a time. More fun starts when you take two at a time and try to match them. So, take the two above inspirational pieces. Think about an annoying project you have in front of you right now. Try this nifty trick using both above proverbs at the same time. Start your annoying project, pay *two* friends to say, "Gee, that's a *good start*," then declare the project done. Two times half-done equals, "Well begun, well done"! Stick with good math.

Most questionable proverbs, though, fall into the category of "Yes, But...." For example,

"Better late than never." *Yes, but...* what about an airplane crash? See, Mr. Smarty-boots, would it not be better for the airplane *never* to crash than to crash *later*? Or how about this popular number:

"A stitch in time saves nine." *Yes, but...* if you're a surgeon in certain specialties, this could get you an extra lawsuit. Or, if you are standing at the edge of a swift jungle river:

"Look before you leap." *Yes, but...* suppose you also see one of those muscular jungle cats sprinting toward you in a bee-lion? Will it be *leap*, or *leopard*? Even if you can't swim, the choice skinnies down.

"Penny wise and pound foolish." *Yes, but...* would it be smart-alecky to notice that some rich genius types refuse to shop at Wal-Mart®? What about that professional driver who disdains self-service gas pumps for his personal vehicle? Can you see **"Pound**

wise and penny foolish" rising to the surface here? After all, three thousand two hundred jars of peanut butter later, Mr. Moneybags would be out a bundle for only shopping at the Superior Golden Polished Peanuts®. Then there are all those dollar bills flushed down the sewer by the A.J. Foyt *wannabe*, who only patronizes the Help-Me-Fill gas station for all eight hundred seventy gallons of fuel each year. Wasteful spendthrifts all, the bums!

"Slow but sure gets there." Good grief, this *Yes, But* can be deadly or just plain bad. Let's say a talent scout in the grocery store spots you majestically picking up a can of peaches and offers you a movie contract, and then you choose to say, "Let me think about it." Or, "Call me tomorrow"?! Wait, let's say that an avalanche comes rolling down the hill at you. No, let's say that your beach day looks ruined when you see a tsunami motoring toward you. Please *do* stop and think slowly about what to do. Your next of kin can tell funny stories about your adventure to pass down generations, and speak your name with reverence. ("Man, I can just see Grandpa high-footing it toward the cabin that used to be on top of that sandy hill—it was 'up one and back two all the way'!")

A very small minority of proverbs do not make any sense at all. How about this anonymous French ditty: **"A silver hammer breaks down an iron door."** What?

I Draw My Revolver

U gly Nazi Hans Johst first claimed that nasty phrase when he reportedly ranted: "When I hear the word culture, I reach for my gun," (later attributed to horrible, chubby, ugly Nazi Hermann Goering). In other words, "People and races and opinions we not like, we shoot." They did. The phrase has been satisfyingly mocked in humorous directions since World War II, most notably by Dr. Stephen Hawking in referring to an irritatingly famous example from quantum theory. We shall continue the tradition here in less technical areas.

Certain words and phrases heard today ought to be condemned outright because they have become so trite that no one listens or even understands the dumb things. Let us put a few out of their deserved misery.

I draw my revolver when I hear: "ta-wenty-fore-seven."

What it really means: "whatever you can do, I already do it better, and all the time."

I sheath my revolver when you say instead: "any time."

I draw my revolver when I hear: "be afraid…"

What it really means: "what I got to say really, really tops anything you can say."

I sheath my revolver when you say instead: "this problem could be interesting."

I draw my revolver when I hear: "surreal."

What it really means: "I heard some Hollywood bozo say it, so it must be cool."

I sheath my revolver when you say instead: [don't say it].

I draw my revolver when I hear: "seriously."
What it really means: "I'm never serious enough the first time I say anything, so I'll just add this cool word to make me more believable this time, I hope."
I sheath my revolver when you say instead: [don't say it].

I draw my revolver when I hear: "up close and personal."
What it really means: "as close as you have to get; I'll stay back here & watch."
I sheath my revolver when you say instead: "close."

I draw my revolver when I hear: "authentic."
What it really means: "Real. But I'm making it more real and much, much cooler."
I sheath my revolver when you say instead: "real" or "actual."

I draw my revolver when I hear: "social justice."
What it really means: "shoveling over some money from people who have it, to others who didn't earn it."
I sheath my revolver when you say instead: [don't say it].

I draw my revolver when I hear: "economic justice."
What it really means: [an honest way to say "social justice"]
I sheath my revolver when you say instead: "cash swap."

I draw my revolver when I hear: "slippery slope."

What it really means: "if I don't like what you say, then 'slippery slope' sounds like a smart put-down, and it could *never* apply to anything I say."

I sheath my revolver when you say instead: [don't say it].

I draw my revolver when I hear: "absolutely." This phrase deserves its own piece, to follow.

I draw my revolver when I hear: "genre." This also deserves its own piece, already done.

I draw my revolver when I hear: "golden."

What it really means: "senior."

I sheath my revolver when …. Hard to say, each year it gets more painful in the shoulder joints.

Being temporarily out of breath and ammunition, and being told by an ugly editor that "enough is enough," I sheath the revolver so we can all get paid. Now I shall listen to the TV for the best source of meaty material on the topic for next time. Shouldn't take long.

Speaking Power to Truth

You're fired!

All right. So you have always heard those title words switched around the other way, *truth* before *power*. Any idea where the original phrase started? Answer: the Quakers, 1955. The American Friends Service Committee (AFSC) published a 70+ page pamphlet titled, "A Quaker Search for an Alternative to Violence," which aimed strong Quaker words at the Cold War politics of the time.

We easily understand the AFSC intentions and aims. Trouble is, the phrase "truth to power" sounded neat to so many other groups since 1955 that they stole the *wordology* for other intentions and aims. Nowadays it's used by noisy, half-organized clusters of persons clomping around business or government buildings, demanding rights for this thing or that. On TV, or course. Here is the real reason almost no one listens, or at least switches channels.

Notice how those people shouting "Truth to power" almost never do so at anyone or anything with much power? Also, these *truths* may be true to *someone*—but not to *many other* people. This is why saying, "Speaking *Power to Truth*" makes *oh*, so much more sense. Take this charming example, back where we started this piece:

Truth: "I don't like working here, the other workers don't want to cooperate with me, so don't blame me if the project doesn't get done."

Power: "You're fired."

See? "Truth" actually speaks a truth, but it matters not a whit to anyone else. How about this historical dandy:

King George III (*Truth*): "You colonial clowns are *blankety blank* English!"

George Washington and colonial clowns (*Power*): "Stuff it up your London Bridge, Georgie."

How about this? *Truthful athlete*: "These drills are stupid."

Powerful coach: "Hey Stupid, you're cut. Better luck next year."

You see? Everyone is speaking truths! Adults will recall Alexander Solzhenitsyn from the 1970s, the Russian activist and author who spoke out loudly about the horrific political prisons in his country of origin, the Soviet Union. A citizen of that country, he was kicked out (fired), came to the U.S. (rehired), and published "GULAG Archipelago." See, now h*ere* was the place to publish his work, not *there*. The international chat likely went thus:

Soviet Union: "Get your ugly Russian butt back here."

Solzhenitsyn: "Kiss ma' ugly butt." Clearly, power had shifted.

Now, going back to that "you're fired" thing, Power could have spoken more soothingly:

Power: "You aren't a bad person. You just don't want to work here."

Can a publisher tell an author, "You're fired"? Are they that powerful? Should I howl back? Should this piece have been left out?

Word Maker

T he word "month" does not have a rhyming word in the English language. Also, I picked up this factoid somewhere, probably a literary or artistic mixer, that no new verbs had been added to the English language recently either. Many nouns have been added, but no verbs except those "-ize" verbs made by plopping *–ize* at the end of nouns often coming from sociology, the economy, and the military. So we have zillions of these unimaginative "new" verbs in English such as, well, *socialize*, *economize*, and *militarize*. As far as "recently" goes, this probably means since Geoffrey Chaucer's day.

Covering both glitches, I now invent a useful new *verb* to rhyme with *month*: "carrunth."

Car•runth'—1. To explode, with a sound like CarrRUUUNTH!; 2. To crumple with intent or by accident; 3. To stomp with seven-league boot; 4. To sound like a cow when chewing a corn cob, or like a cow eight hours after digesting said corn cob.

Speaking of Chaucer, think how much better his Prologue to *Canterbury Tales'* opening lines could have been with this useful new word. He had composed:

"Whan that aprill with his shoures soote
The droghte of march hath perced to the roote,
And bathed every veyne in swich licour
Of which vertu engendred is the flour;"

Good grief, what is he saying? Consider swapping this clear two-liner instead:

"Whan them shoures break through aprill month,
Farmer stompet alle floures *carrunth*;"

Chaucer could have added a Farmer's Tale to that epic, to boot.

Now take this famous gem from poet Robert Burns. Change his memorable stanza thus:

"But Mousie, thou art no thy lane,
In proving foresight every month:
The best-laid schemes o' mice an' men
Gang aft *carrunth*,"

Today it's Chaucer and Burns, tomorrow: Shakespeare! Unfortunately, the editor will not permit more space being taken for antiquities, but you get the idea. A modern business couplet might run like this:

"With the bills pouring in at the end of the month,
Accountants at the business in unison carrunth."

The next step will be to send a proposal to the Dictionary Police to add this valuable new verb to the English language. There is a good chance that they will carrunth my letter.

Conversions

How to start a great family fight: what is the real meaning of *conversion*—in football? Is it one of those third down nail biters, or is it the added point or points after a touchdown? Does it involve a kicking play, or a running play? If all three, which came first? That is, what is the real, original meaning of *conversion* in football? Does it matter in a sort of important way? Problems, problems, so many thoughtful teasers taking up our time.

All right, *conversions* might also remind us experienced guys of that old movie, "12 Angry Men." This story turns around a criminal trial jury deliberating over a murder charge, and boasting a famous cast of at least twelve, but if you watched it, then you will remember two things.

First, it was hot, humid and rainy as these hyped juror-actors sweated through the drama, wondering if they could remember all their lines to "avoid another damn camera retake." Second, the story line roughly spent an hour or so with the various jurors trying to convert the others to their point of view and verdict. Everyone *in the know* knew that Henry Fonda would win out in the end. People were converted back and forth to make the movie interesting, and to make sure the movie lasted a full couple hours for all the honest ticket payers.

Aside from these fake, play-act conversions, we should be concerned about three more quite *real* ones. One of the most important, as you strongly suspect, involves the conversion of English to metric. You know, "I wouldn't touch that with a nine foot pole" becomes, "I wouldn't touch that with a 2.74320 meter pole."

Poetic, no? Many more interesting conversions happen from old English to regular English. Our favorite from college technical days was converting a velocity (speed) from *miles per hour* to *furlongs per fortnight.* With a slide rule. Now what might the answer be?

A second other-important conversion involves switching political parties. Common wisdom tells us that once a convert, the brain morphs to inflexible. Sociologists have named this phenomenon *devout secular blatherblinding.* The name was invented to stop further phenomenon naming by renegade sociologists. Political parties, therefore, should immediately begin a strategy to convert all persons to their party. They will be wise to use a time-honored and effective strategy: beer. Mind you, this cannot be a watery suds-in-a-barrel offering. An earlier time-honored strategy of simply paying people was also quite effective, until the jail time got too long.

A third kind of other-conversion includes everything else philosophers can dream up in their ample free time, and creates the greatest angst. One of these we can speak about here is folding your hands the "opposite" way. If you don't "get it," clasp your hands in front of you right now. Either your left thumb or your right thumb in on the outside (closest to you). Now clasp your hands the opposite way. *Ha, ha, ha* you say, *no big deal.* The "big deal" is doing it when no one is looking, reverently. Converting, therefore, means: can you opposite-clasp without guilt or backsliding?

Here are the sorts of things that will determine if you are "taking this to heart." While opposite-clasping, can you figure out what species of bird is doing that odd tweeting from a tree 80 feet away? What about planning the protein food for your next cookout? What would you name the next flavor of Cadbury egg? Why are you holding your hands clasped opposite so hard?

The answer to that last question has to do with some wise sage with a smooth voice and temporal authority over you—me!—raising your consciousness with a challenge. If you do not answer carefully, sagely, in a reasonable time but not too long, then you will be seen as a washy, wasting wimp. Never mind that there is utterly no one else around. Because I asked you all those questions, *you* made up the audience. "Why do I not cross my fingers opposite" creates its own truth *and epistemology* here that you have to adopt, adapt, or drop! Your likely answer to this important question? "Maybe I could change, but I forgot the other questions anyway."

Oh yes, that *furlongs* thing: there are exactly 2,688 furlongs per fortnight for each mile-per-hour. Use this useful conversion with grace and humor at your next engineering or scientific mixer....

Running for Office

"**M**y fellow Americans, I am speaking to you tonight so that we may better understand the crisis in which we find ourselves. The overwhelming environmental influences into which the economic activity constrains us makes it difficult to tackle our many pressing problems.

"The policies of the past will no longer lead us into the future. The future belongs, must belong, to those who are willing to step up to the plate and take action.

"We need only follow the money to discover the root causes of problems we now all face. Now is no time for partisan political stances, no time to posture over positions which have neither worked, nay, can never work under any circumstance.

"Campaign rhetoric will not suffice to end the stalemates and move the ball forward. We simply cannot allow partisan agendas get in our way any longer.

"Too often, tired old political points interfere with the movement toward improvements the American people crave. The answers clearly lie in the wholeness of the stillness of the nation and the world, *vis a vis* the community. If we act together to go to page 2...

"(Wup)

"... uh, if we act together to bring this great country to the balance which we have historically achieved, and made a difference to ourselves, our neighbors, and our allies, then once again we shall show the greatness to which we were heir.

"All of you hard working citizens out there deserve better than this. Too many others of privilege find ways to get breaks that you can't. In another age, this would be called 'corruption.' 'Graft.' 'Cheating the system.' I will no longer tolerate this situation.

"I speak to you lastly about a crisis of daily mounting proportion, and about which we must act now and with energy. *Chickens.* Yes, our chickens have been losing protein, and thereby threaten the nutrition of our entire nation. This intolerable situation cannot stand. We must begin now to restore our chickens to their former fat greatness.

"Yes, we must begin TODAY to right this terrible problem. I demand, 'A POT ON EVERY CHICKEN!!'"

Ceteris Paribus

"Please be seated at the back of the bus." At first, I thought that's what the foreign phrase meant. It was never intended as a racial thing back in grade school, but rather a little-kid thing. See, in my day, the little kids had to go to the back of the school bus, and sit three to a seat. Gads! I really hated that, but our bus driver seemed like a nice person, and she spoke with some kind of accent. Anyway, the darned phrase keeps showing up enough to be annoying, so I thought I should find out some day what it meant or where it came from.

As a young adult, I gave the phrase scant thought, though I laughed about, "See the terraces of Paris by bus." Had I noted that it popped up from time to time in my mathematics books, and that I never actually consulted a travel agent, then the silly idea would never have rooted in.

One day, at least I finally found out for sure that this foreign ditty came from Greek. A friend sitting next to me at a meeting suspected that I cheated and looked up the phrase, or just plain made the whole thing up. Not so, and here's how it happened. That previous week I saw some out-of-country tourists in Washington, D.C., returning to their tour transport area, and one of the older men with "BROOKLYN, NY" on the front of his T-shirt was pointing and told his group, "...see *deez* pair of buses." The back of his T-shirt read, "I'm Greek to Me!" Well, that was good enough for me too, and all at once this settled the matter.

My editor later grumbled something like "Latin, not Greek, if you say it right," but you already read about un-smart this guy was. All else being equal, I still do not know precisely what *ceteris paribus* means, but I figured out its origin.

Caucus

D o they cuss at a political caucus? (Why do we %$^#%!!@# go through this every four years? When do we %$^#%!!@# get to go to the bar? Dang, it's %$^#%!!@# hot in here! %$^#%!!@#!!!). No wonder. These presidential convention brain-drags are kind of like an old East Bloc annual Party spectacle, without the nine hour butt-numbing, endless yak about false production figures. Instead, at our presidential convention caucuses you get nine individual one-hour butt-numb'ers about false promises.

So, exactly where does the term *caucus* come from, and how has it moved on from *there* to *here*? Like everything else, watch how easy it is to make a short story long…. First, note that *caucus* does have a Latiny sound to it. Those Latins reportedly did have a drinking cup by that name back then, but there is no way such a silly word could end up applying to such a *serious* event like a presidential convention.

A little vigorous research has uncovered the origin as *Russian*. Few have bothered noticing the similarity of the word to the Caucasus region somewhere around southern Russia, near the Caspian Sea. Most of my readers who do not recognize either place will rush to the globe at this point to satisfy their insatiable thirst for knowledge. Hint: "Caspian" is easier to find than "Caucasus"; put your finger on the Caspian Sea, and look immediately to the left. Anyway, the connection between the two words is compelling. Ph.D. candidates in, oh, just about everything like to use the phrase, "…connection is compelling." Follow this simple, but compelling trail.

First, "Caucasus" is not plural—you have *a* Caucasus region. Second, what do you call people from there? Russian? Probably not. Caucasian? Yes, but not any longer. Clearly, those original people scattered long ago because of the environment—the air was polluted with ancient Russian spear points. A Ph.D. candidate a couple centuries or so ago, though, made a compelling case for naming a major branch of Homo sapiens "Caucasians," because that region seemed like the center of where people with whitish-looking skins started out.

His Ph.D. thesis has long since disappeared, or burned up, or been used for wrapping old beef scraps, though we importantly do know of the author's major line of proof. To summarize, put a tack in your globe at the Caucasus region, the stretch a string from that point in both east and west directions, and you will find Caucasian persons located equally in both directions. Astonishing! This discovery came to be called the *Caucasian String Theory*. Such powerful reasoning obviously earned this Ph.D. candidate a doctorate. Or at least a tall beer, served in a Latin caucus.

Our modern story of *caucus* supposedly began along the Atlantic coast of the North American colonies a couple hundred years ago. Many American colonists were scuffling with Britain, and with each other, about how to spend their free time over the next millennium. So, ask yourself these two questions:

Did this colonial area lie along the Caucasian String?

Were these early scuffling colonials Caucasian?

The answer to both is a resounding "Yes!" In fact, some critics today of the Founding Fathers claim that they were "just a bunch of old white men wearing Caucasian wigs."

The next step becomes iffier, because the origin of *caucus* is attributed a person of high moral character who was unlikely to have actually spoken the word. You see, we think that *caucus* became a contraction of "Caucasians cussing," because those scuffling colonial political meetings produced room-purpling amounts of very bad words from a lot of colonial Caucasian men. First it was *Cau'cussing*, then contracted further to *cau'cuss*, and then the contraction and one "S" was dropped and became the *caucus* of today.

The person of high moral character in question was *The* John Adams of Braintree, Mass., and such a man would not speak this way about a wild scene of cussing and drinking. What he *wouldn't*, nay *couldn't* do, was use contractions in his speech. Somebody did, though, and John Adams was the last to get stuck with it, sort of like the game of "Not-It!"

So here we are, having solved another curious word origin. As mentioned, there likely has already been a Ph.D. awarded on the topic, so this essay merely uncovers a *very* convenient truth. Future political conventions will now be easier to watch, even through all the multiple one-hour butt-numbing promises. Sit back, and fill a large Latin "caucus" with your favorite hops-based beverage, and check off how many times you mumble at the TV, "Yeah, right, you butt-numbing horse's butt." Then sing the Political Convention Song before turning in for the night:

> I cuss
> You cuss
> We all cuss
> At caucuses

It turns out that Southern Russian Region people could sing the same song, if they don't mind the bad spelling. They can pour vodka, though, in their Latin caucuses. Same size caucus.

Barcarolle

I t's good to have a cherished mate sitting by your side when you are staring at a musical program, wondering how some of the pieces got titled as they did. Shortly we would find out as the virtuoso will arrive on stage, and perform a *barcarolle*. What, we ask, was the plain original meaning of "barcarolle"?

This time, instead of my usual learned and penetrating analysis, I lurched toward stupid. "What da' hell is a barcarolle," I opined sophisticatedly. Brightening, I continued, "Wait! A barcarolle is when you buy a sack of chocolate bark, then roll 'em up and sell as logs, or smoke 'em!"

Ugh.

"How are you going to roll a slab of chocolate into anything?" she says. "It doesn't bend". "No, wait! "Barcarolle" is when you take one of those yappy little kick-dogs to the top of a snowy hill, then roll him down, head over butt!"

Thud.

"O.K., you don't use chocolate for your barcarolle," I piled on excitedly in a loud whisper, "you bundle up a bunch of sycamore sheddings, put 'em in a Kaiser bun, and get your *barcarolle* with mustard and tomato and a large beer!"

Double-thud.

"No, no wait -- you know those loud chubby guys with a cane that promote circus acts?" Her turn was next. "A *barker-roll* is what he carries on his stomach!"

Ooooo.

Mercifully, the pianist smiled onto center stage and performed a perfect Chopin "Barcarolle." That kick-dog thing was still pretty funny.

Tweet

@whaddeverthuhel

If U don't follow me U wont hear if I really do have purple undies 2day. Inside info sez buy stock B4 merge 2morrow 230PM, NASDQ symbol: C_,

+++++++

1st to hold a B-flat for 12 min continuous on bass bassoon & email attach winz $5000, pls verify addr, org/photo creds, call first 212-465-3

State of the Union

"**M**y fellow Americans...."
Those words are the best part of these annual rituals. This hour-plus speech should be called the "State of the Onion." Why? Because the presidents' talks over the last century have had to cover topic after topic after layered topic—you peel away one, and there's another! Also, these events bring stinging tears to your eyes, wondering when you can turn off your TV.

The president really does have to end up yakking about many topics, because if he doesn't touch this base or that, the jawing, then second, third and fourth guessing by pundits and newspapers goes on and on for weeks. Might as well jaw a little extra from the dais. So the president's talk is like trying to run with a paper bag full of warm water to the barrel before the bag breaks.

On the other brilliant hand, the U.S. Constitution only requires the president to "...from time to time give to the Congress Information of the State of the Union...." This "information" traditionally was done by sending an annual *written* letter to Congress, until one of those puffy presidential advisors, Cornelius L. Windbreaker, insisted that his boss do the deed in person, and verbosely. Historical Mistake. Now we are stuck. Whether by speech or by letter, by land or by sea, the president's message gets stretched out anyway. Make life easy for you and us, Mr. President! Shorten everyone's tedium. Send it in writing once again.

The following short and equally meaningless statements could show up in a brief *written* State of the Union:

"Foreign policy should flourish with our foreign friends."

"Domestic policy should dominate our dear domiciles."

"Alliterations should alleviate otherwise awful answers."

"Leaves should be mulched."

Oh, just turn on the TV in February. You need to say that you heard it.

The World is Awash in Content

Where in blazes did that phrase come from? After a modest amount of online research, we see the annoying thing showing up every year as we delve back and back and back in time into the 1980s. In fact, it pops up as far as when online researching started. What a coincidence! This phrase *itself* has now also become awash in content. All the e-hits on that phrase bring up some-gloomy-body or other moaning about how many words, how much stuff (undefined) is "out there"—that means *public*, we can guess.

What most of these loudmouths mean: not just sportscasters, but also all kinds of occupations and businesses have too many people in them! That would be bad for dancers, film producers, singers, mimes, sportswriters, accountants, actors, financial advisers, college students, electromagnetic interference (EMI) engineers and scientists, restaurants, and politicians. In short, just about everybody, even authors. In good economic times, every field has persons and companies surviving at the fringes.

Think of the most recent ugly restaurant meal you ate, for example. When times get tighter, this establishment disappears. When times get better, you get more restaurants, good ones and still more ugly ones. See? The fringes will always be with us!

Then suddenly a need pops up, say, in the electromagnetic interference (EMI) field of expertise when a crazed Central Equatorial African Republic Air Force pilot fires off a small surprise nuclear explosion off the coast of Virginia. Now the ordinary, fringe EMI engineers will get fat consulting jobs because the field suddenly just got bigger, and newer EMI engineers form *new* fringes. Sigh.

"Awash in content" sounds like the grumbling of persons who just ate a bad lunch, actually. Now, to prove that "content" can be an exciting thing, though, consider these topics that have little or no content yet, and which some ambitious person can expand, then become rich and noticed:

- Pizza service on Baffin Island
- "Winning draw poker strategies for unemployed terrorists"
- Monogramming llamas

Oh, now let's not be silly here! No one would invest a moment's effort investigating those fascinating, but hopeless topics. All right, then. Have a look at these heavyweight, serious topics:

- Inventing the internal combustion pogo stick
- A history of Hungarian ski jumpers
- "Genghis Khan invented hip hop"
- Rhinoceros polo

Important Note No. 1: of course, by the time my tens of thousands of readers try looking up those seven topics, the number of new articles and hits will multiply exponentially. This will be directly caused by all you busy research fanatics. So it would be smart to look for other items *less* awash with assorted content. Be creative! By the way, do not say "exponentially" to real mathematicians. Say "lots" instead. These preachy folks will remind you that, when you don't know squat, "short words is better grammar."

Important Note No. 2: Henry Ford. Old Henry scolded an interviewer long ago by telling him—telling the *world*, "...no field is overcrowded with talent!" All right, so I can't find the quote in any of my touted online research, but rather it was passed down three generations through my family of Ford automobile fanatics, so it must be true. Even if not exactly quoted, the old man's challenge could not be stronger or truer. Look at the zillions of successful persons, past and present—all fields, even sportscasters—how they worked hard and kept at it.

Important Note No. 3, cheaters: Mao Tse-Tung. He wrote up a dozen plays (all variations of his same exciting theme, we have heard) and his notorious Little Red Book, all of which made him a millionaire. Since Mao was the only author allowed in China at that time, and his productions were the only such diversions permitted, his competition was light and his income was as heavy as his dessert plate. His play productions were supposedly always packed (or else!).

Maybe no one will pick up the ball and run with any of these seven topics of mine, but everyone has a story that must get out. Maybe I should keep that hot list on my desk top....

Absolutely? Absolutely Not!

D o you remember the CEO of GE Capital who was being interviewed on TV about his highly public divorce in the late 1990s? That CEO was Gary Wendt, the top GE Capital man. More memorable was his answer to the question about doing a prenuptial contract next time, IF he ever decided to get married again. He smiled at the camera, nodded his round head, and answered, "**ab'**-so-**lu'**-te-ly!" Twice. Absolutely *what*? A simple "yes" would have done nicely—and more accurately. GE Capital is that company who sent you credit card offers in the mail back then. These days they are more into commercial credit, and quite successfully so. Mr. Wendt made his fortune running the corporation and the then-Mrs.-Wendt eventually made quite a few bucks as well.

The interview with Mr. Gary Wendt did point out how much "absolutely" gets used by just about everybody. You can hear famous people every day being interviewed, reaching for the A-word like a spare tool strapped to their microphones. Goodness, listen to politicians from all over creation stumbling over each other trying to out-*absolutely* the others.

Congresspersons from both sides of the Washington Capitol aisle are notorious for being *absolutely sure* that Western Civilization will come crashing down immediately if their bills do not pass into law, and *right now*. Sadly, the minor political parties and other odd public talking heads picked up the habit.

At both the Emmy and Academy Awards red carpets, you would run out of fingers and toes counting the A-words coming from the mouths of all those stars.

No doubt, though, one of the best harvesting grounds for the A-word is cable and network TV, all competing for the largest crop of A-worders from the dozen talking panels they cook up for us every day. Tune in and keep a scorecard. Bring two pencils. But wait! You could do this at an average gathering of average persons these days.

Why do we use the A-word? To impress our listeners. How else could that poor listener understand how clever we are? Clearly, we feel a desperate need to crown our sentence with a big four-syllable bully word. Remember the *owwwooogah* of a Model "T" horn piercing a theater's dark calm when Ma & Pa Kettle drove up to the house in that 1949 movie? That old horn *owwwooogah* rhymes well with "*AB-so-Loooooootly*"! The horn sounds smarter.

There are good ways to avoid saying *AB-so-Loooooootly.* Consider these four easy tricks:

• Trick #1: Substitute "yes":
"Was Einstein the best in his field?" Bad answer: "absolutely."
"Hi, Joe. Did you enjoy the movie yesterday?" Bad answer: "absolutely."
"Will you vote next election differently?" Bad answer: (oh, you know!)
"Yes" takes three fewer syllables and less breath. With less hot air floating around, think how this would help out global warming.

• Trick #2: Substitute "no" for "absolutely not":
"Senator, did you know that your campaign account didn't.....?" Etc. Bad answer: "absol-oooote-ly not."

You get the idea here, too. It's four fewer syllables this time. A qualified "maybe" instead of "no" might also be a good answer to the question and does not run the risk of backing you into a future corner after answering "absolutely not." It is harder for that senator to be called out later if he had simply answered "maybe."

• Trick #3: Substitute "very," with or without some other sparkling adverb.

Now don't go soft. It is tempting to say "that pie was *absolutely* good!" or, "we saw a monument that was *absolutely* huge," or, "that was the *absolutely* worst book I ever read." You could have said "very" instead. The trouble with using "very," though, is that the word has about as much color as floodwater, but none of the energy. Still, how about saying, "great pie," a "huge monument," or "the worst book"; which are actually:

• Trick #4: how about saying *nothing at all*? Leave the A-word out! Not using the A-word at all will do most of the time nicely. *Owwwooooooooooogah.*

There are exceptions. The "A" word's *adjective* cousin—"absolute"—has a long and respectable history. *Absolute* zero, *absolute* vacuum, *absolute* numbers are indispensable terms in science and mathematics. Picture yourself in a classroom with Dr. Richard Feynman. Do not in any circumstance ask him to say "*yes* numbers" or "*very* numbers," or you will find yourself punched in the hypotenuse. After you have heard the umpteenth movie star answer *absolutely*, through the chomp of their chewing gum, you are from now on guaranteed to either cringe or laugh. Laughter shows better form.

Yes, there are exceptions even for the A-word itself. *Absolutely* implies an oath, a promise of truth. *Absolutely* should promise that you can count on whatever follows. Here's a good and thoroughly accurate example: if you feel the devil in you rising to the surface, trying to force you to use the A-word, then ABSOLUTELY the *last word* here is great advice: ***don't***!

What's in a Name?

W e found out how hard it is to be green earlier. Now, here's something easy. *Três* easy: being Aaron Zyzur. They make movies with titles like, "Being Aaron Zyzur."

Picture this flashback. A lucky little boy strolls into the candy store, puts his name on the list for the free candy handout the kindly proprietor holds as a promotion each week. This week, the kindly proprietor goes in alpha order, and guess which name pops up first, hands down?

As long as little Aaron puts his first name, then last name, no one, but no one beats "Aaron." Were he a showoff and instead put down his middle name, Yulzileiner (a family name for seven generations), it would be "no candy for you," little A.Z.! In practice, average candy store proprietors would not pick a winner using alpha-order. Otherwise, he would get suspicious when chubby little Aaron walked out with the candy parcel 15 weeks in a row. In practice, few or no candy store proprietors would offer such a promotion anyway.

Now switch the picture twelve years ahead. Little Aaron has now become Recruit Aaron, US Army. The game is the same, but the prizes differ somewhat. When it comes time to list out "volunteering" tasks, Big Aaron clearly jots his name down, "Zyzur, Aaron." You see, the chances of being alpha-picked are now greater and riskier in the Service than they ever were in childhood. The recruit needs to be prepared. You could not find a farther-down name than Zyzur, even with a ten minute head start, even with a five dollar bet. In practice, Aaron's risk is still large in the Service. His platoon sergeant could mess things up by posting the list upside down.

True enough, you can't pick either your name or your relatives (or the color of the used car you want to buy). If the luck of the name-draw gives you "Aaron Zyzur," you still need to be limber and flexible to maximize the opportunities life will hand you. You can be first or last, your choice.

Take the above candy store example. The prudent child Aaron Zyzur will snoop around a bit before entering the freebie contest to make sure, utterly sure, that the weekly prize doesn't end up being licorice. Licorice jellybeans. What a *godawful* way to start the weekend, with a sack of medicine candy. He would even have to thank the kindly proprietor on the way out the store.

Here's What the "Others" Are Here For:

L inus van Pelt, in that old Peanuts cartoon, gets credit for asking, "What are we here for?" after which Lucy, his sister, tells him that we are put on earth "to help others." Lucy was certainly not the first to say that. This famous phrase has been claimed by many others (not the same "others") long, long before Lucy. I forget who the real bonehead in history gets the first-finder credit, but we shall see who the *real* originator likely was. It goes back to the days of early fire people.

See, there was this hunter—not named "Thag," as you might think, but definitely thag-lookalike—who first mumbled the "...others..." phrase in disgust, even though he couldn't write it down. He couldn't speak it well either.

He had spent two days chasing an antler-bearing herbivore, finally cornering and scuffling with it for an hour or two, receiving numerous antler wounds before subduing it. Then he dragged it back "home," taking about a half day, then skinning, de-gutting, and more or less cutting it into steaks sized for carnivores.

After having to start a fire himself, put up with six little thags asking "Are we there yet?" plus one thag-mate complaining about the mess on her cooking rocks, he starting grilling the "meat" over his fire. It was at this point that a tight group of sweet-smelling thagish relatives started crowding around the fire. Grilled herbivore steaks got all kinds of folks like that excited back then.

Actually, the Hero Hunter grumbled, "I know what these mooching cousins are here for." He had the good grace not to call them "Others," but there they were, and he "was here to help them." Humanity got off on the wrong barefoot right about then, give or take a few dozen thousand years. Had our man the brilliance of a CEO, or better, a Barcelona stevedore, he could have done us all a great favor by making one of these forceful announcements:

- "Anyone will be entitled to his own steak if he or she goes out and brings back a cookable green leaf. The bringer-backer will, of course, have to show that he or she can keep down the first three mouthfuls; or,
- "The same deal—if a dessert is furnished. Do not bring moose manure pie; or,
- "The same deal—if anyone will write down the herbivore steak recipe." This means that said genius would have to invent an *app*, along with some kind of writing tool and medium. Somebody that smart might even come up with grammar rules and Esperanto (not at the same time). If successful, then this precocious brat should be exiled right after the meal. We wouldn't want a literate nut job around to write lies about the history of all this.

This caper would not work, of course. A few clever steak holders will sneakily survive long enough to write the whole thing up, excluding the part about the Hero having to catch and bring home the antlered bacon. Being one of the Others then gets forever portrayed as thoughtful, smart, patient, generous (giving passing credit to the sweet-smelling, but unnamed game hunter), articulate, family minded, brave, thoughtful... oh, we said that one before... citizen of Thagworld. Otherwise, and to boot, the Others end up with fewer antler wounds.

An aside: the word "Other-wise" comes down to us from all this history.

An Easy Answer

Scott Adams, creator of the unsurpassed cartoon series Dilbert, lobbied in one of his columns to simplify the three homonyms "there," "their," and "they're." In it, he pushes for the English grammar dictators just to pick one of those three for use in all cases. He cares not a whit which one gets picked, but that we end up with only one. Great idea!

Maybe not. This is where things get really nasty. Very quickly we would have a national "Save *Their* National Butts," a nonprofit, fundraising at the usual appropriate dinner telemarketing hour. TV would air the new action drama series, "They're Coming for Your *They're*." Home-grown Ciceros in the park would be haranguing passersby with howling, colorful "*There* Be the Fools!" Congresspersons would be heard arguing in their (woops) usual principled chuff for whichever of these three words had 50.1% of their (oh, damn!) constituents' backing.

I have an easy, though not too elegant way out of this. Now, Einstein had said something about simplifying an explanation as far as you can, but no further. Or something like that. Also, famous journalist H.L. Mencken had quipped that every complex problem has solutions that are simple, neat, and wrong. Or something like that. No, Mr. Einstein, my brilliant idea can't be simplified further. Sorry also, H.L., but we bag you too, because the triple-thār(e) problem is *not* complex by any stretch. To be fair, Mencken didn't exactly say that phrase either.

I credit old Arkansas Clem with the inspiration for my jewel of an answer. Simply substitute "thar" for all three troublesome thār's. "*Thar* they go, with *thar* ugly cousin to get a *harrcut*, and *thar* comin' back at fi'thirty." See? Thar's an answer that's simple, neat, and just feels right.

All right, no bad words about Poppy's choice of words. It's obviously already written anyway. You will now see his vast business experience shouting at you, so merely head into the next important area....

.

A WORD ABOUT BUSINESS

Hearing Problems

"*What'sreallypissesmeoff....*" I half-heard over my left shoulder somewhere, while sitting at a lunch table halfway through this all-day business conference, scribbling some notes from the morning, and already half-annoyed by that inconsiderate boob howling into his cell phone three tables over.

"Me too," I grumbled to someone standing next to me. Then I turned to my left and saw this well-dressed, smiling gentleman extending his hand and introducing himself.

"Wassily. Wassily Pismiyov. I am going to lead the one o'clock seminar, and I saw you in the last session at nine-thirty."

Oops.

Very few times I am gifted with recovering quickly, and this was one of them. A lucky thing, because Dr. Pismiyov is not only a well-respected monetary consultant, but also clearly has a kindly sense of humor. Quickly standing and shaking his hand, I complimented him on his career and the value of the seminar program, and about how I am certainly *not* Wassily Pismiyov, and must have been mumbling to myself like a dreamy fool a few seconds ago. After all, I didn't admit that some people call me *Poppy*.

The good Doctor P. pretended not to have heard me babble. We chatted amiably about the nine-thirty session, mostly about metal-based currencies, real deflation, and foreign exchange. Really interesting stuff. Actually, really boring stuff, if you have any sense. I did grouse, though, about Mr. _____'s draggy talk on the history of the U.S. dollar.

Dr. Wassily reminded me, "Well, you want the dollar wild and volatile, or monotone and reliable?"

He got me there. I also grumbled about how these sessions would be more dignified if there weren't so many in the room who were inhaling Styrofoam cartons of fast food during the program. Mostly french fries, I think. For breakfast.

"I suppose so, but it's guys like that who pay our bills," he reminded me, "they buy lots of tickets to these programs!"

Yup. For sure.

Then old *Yak-a-Boy* on his cell phone, three tables over, upped his volume to a five-table reach, and both the Doctor P. and I kind of looked over that way. Wassily, my new and interesting friend, who saw my growly face at this loud goofball, chimed in with almost no trace of his Slavic accent:

"Yah, I know. Those inconsiderate boobs really piss me off."

The Ant and the Grasshopper

ÆSOP, the Fable Guy, has always gotten good press, but a bad rap. These days we remember that *Ae* guy who told short tales of animals, with and without tails, each ending with a preachy moral. Those morals always seemed so dry and unpretty; sayings like:

"Hope not to succeed in borrowed plumes."
"It is wise not to be too greedy."
"Pride goes before destruction."
"See not your friends before morning coffee."

An Aesop with an attitude like that must have been real fun over a beer.

It's the cranky tenor of these sayings that have given the gent the bad rap. Take the story of the ant and the grasshopper. It came passed down to us with a rather stark ending, and one which sounds pretty rough to us moderns. There was this ant who worked her butt off each summer day carrying grains and greens from a farmer's field back to her pantry and back again, all day long.

The grasshopper, happily chirping and singing in the fields, chided the ant on her way by because she worked so hard all the time. "Come out here and sing and dance and enjoy the beautiful summer," called he after her. But the ant plodded on her way, busily storing up food for the winter.

Winter arrived, snowy and cold, with all the vegetable food either dead or covered up. With nothing to eat, and not feeling much like singing, the grasshopper hopped to the ant's hole and knocked on her door (don't ask). Summarizing the colorful dialog which followed, the ant told him to get lost, and where he could stuff his sheet music. The End of The Story.

MORAL: Don't hit your ant up for money in the winter when you've been ragging on her all summer. Something like that.

Now why, oh why do they blame poor Aesop with so-called fables like that? Vigorous research again has uncovered the truth, that old Aesop actually owned and ran the family horse farm. It was never *Aesop's Fables*. It's *Aesop's Stables*. He was an unequaled businessman and ranted all his life about practicing basic good business ethics, even when horse trading. Here's how his grasshopper tale really went.

It is true that the ant went back & forth a million times storing up food in her pantry, and it is also true that the grasshopper sang his buns off all day while the ant carried stuff to her ant hole. Each time the ant went by, though, the grasshopper did get a twinge about taking some time off to put away a treat or two for later. At the time, there were enough snacks around to munch on after a busy day of singing, so the grasshopper kept putting that extra task on his to-do list for the next day.

The ant also thought about other matters than simply dragging eats back home. That silly grasshopper *did* have a large repertoire, and he really was quite a good crooner. "It's hot work dragging all this future food around, and I should rest for a while with all that good entertainment in the air." At the time, though, that goofy green fool was always singing, so it was not like one couldn't pause and listen any time. She again put that resting stop idea on her to-do list for the next day.

Winter. Yes, the grasshopper did realize his mistake in not piling up a stack of grasshopper swag when the stuff was just lying around in the warm weather. He also realized that he could not handle a shovel. How was he supposed to know that? The life expectancy of his species did not extend to much past the last winter. This was a horrible time to be a hungry grasshopper with no paying audience.

Meanwhile, the ant, having snugged herself into her ant hole, plenty of ant chow all around, pondered on how interesting her life turned out to be. "What shall I do today? Let's see, eat a seed? My, this is going to be fun. Like yesterday, and tomorrow, and the day after that." This was a horrible time to be a bored ant with no MP3 player.

A knock at the ant's door came none too soon for either species.

This sensible arrangement did have rough spots, of course, as there will be with any business arrangement. One of those happened with the food trade deal, Aesop tells us. It turns out that the ant's larder was weighted toward the grains, but the grasshopper's tastes leaned toward green and leafy vegetables. "Oho," says the ant, "that'll run you extra. I'm saving the grasses for the occasional desserts I serve."

"All right," bargained the grasshopper," I shall sing one more of those longer pieces per week. Let's say, an old rock group you like, such as Pink Floyd in concert, OR one more Mozart opera, full instrumental. Large weeds for lunch, then?" And so arrangements were struck, both ant and grasshopper coming out much happier for the deals.

MORAL: One is wise to avoid being either too fanatically antsy or *unhoppy*.

ALTERNATE MORAL: One who keeps busy trading has no time to become chubby.

IRRELEVANT FACT: The old storyteller's business tagline was, "You don't horse around with such a chubby deal at Aesop's Stables."

What's with strutting this "Ae" stuff anyway, Aesop? Technically, it teases even some otherwise smart moderns to spell common words oddly, such as *aesthetics*, *aeon*, *aether*, and *Aethiopia*. Why be British and waste the "A"?

Team Building

F or some reason people seem to like that famous catch-me-while-I-fall-down-backwards exercise which team-building consulting geniuses load into their *motivational* seminars. One person has to fall backwards ramrod straight, whilst his trusted teammates catch him before smacking into the floor, backwards. This drill supposedly builds good, trusting teams, but more likely just proves that sane people avoid going to jail for letting a comrade wham his head on the floor. We assume everyone takes a turn being the trusting backward-faller person. For a medium sized team, full participation stretches out the drill for larger swag payments to the consultant. This also builds a very loyal consulting team.

I, for one, do not care so much if my team "has my back," as long as they hold onto my ugly head. Never worry about *independent misanthropes* showing up on the team. Misanthropes, as we have seen, choose their company carefully and would not likely throw good cash money at silly seminars featuring this kind of dawdling. In truth, almost all of these drills end up as exercises in avoiding personal humiliation.

It won't take an Immanuel Kant to see that avoiding embarrassment is the best practical team builder. It's the cheapest one, if you have to hire consultants. Besides the humiliation, most of these events feel sort of like eating whipped cream pies. The first bite might fool half the people with a thirty-second sugar high. The rest of the day drudges down to finishing the pies without either looking foolish or throwing up. Throwing up would look foolish also.

The best team building program would be *none at all* if great people were hired in the first place, of course. Assuming you are stuck with a "team" who have sort of randomly ended up over time in a loosely related bunch, though, you have better ways for doing a team building. Consider these three alternative gems:

#1—Instead of signing up for an actual "team building" or "company motivational" seminar (*Humiliation City*), pick instead any old inexpensive two-day business or cultural program that features a knock-out buffet. Give your team a goal of swiping enough quality eats from the goodies tables to supply the whole team for the next entire day for free. The most productive *swiper* gets first pick of the desserts brought back.

#2—Do not go for one of those pricey "outward bound" deals. You do not want to waste time with the men showing off their Abercrombie's, or the women their Birkenstocks. Instead, go to a sports bar on a mid-late Thursday afternoon and spread the team into two spots. One gloms onto the bar, and the other clusters loosely on an adjacent table. More or less half the crew goes to each, and the makeup of the two groups matters not. No, they do not play swipe-the-snacks this time. This day of the week and this time of day are ideal to group-think-talk about what seven actions the company or nonprofit should launch headlong into during the next month. Each. Call these seven bullets or items, "Brilliants." At some point, the two half-teams swap places, look over the other group's seven *Brilliants*, and add three more *Brilliants*. Each.

At some even later point, the two half-teams mingle and bandy about the total of 20 new *Brilliants*.

Do not agonize, just bandy. Pick three *Brilliants*, preferably by using darts tossed from five feet into the charted list of *Brilliants*. Teams will be astonished how much good stuff flows from this relatively cheap afternoon. You see, those other costly outward-bound things get everybody hyped for, well, being outside. Thereafter, the exhausted team will be hyped for a nap. This end point is exactly what the outward bound program sought to avoid.

#3—Finding out, in some detail, what each team member gets personally excited about will get your team fired up better than the above two. In fact, do this anyway. Ask each person to tell the group something about themselves—what they might be doing or creating—that no one else likely knows about. I have found this to rank head 'n shoulders above any other team building drill.

Schemes 1 and 2 might actually work, but number 3 here has important information to let others in the team know about. It also costs only bottled water and bagels, and the team members won't even notice these. No big seminar fee, no bar bill, no bored or humiliated team builders. Every person—every last one—will talk clearly and animated about something very, very important to themselves personally. Faces will glow. Say that about one of those meetings where folks talk about "organizational vision"? Hah! No contest!

That Silly 80-20 Rule

Y ou've likely heard about this thing many times. If not, the 80-20 Rule goes something like this: "In *all groups*, 80% of the results get done by the top 20% of the people." This cutie also belonged to the "I Draw My Revolver" piece. A small amount of small arithmetic has to follow, but you don't mind a bit of minor math, do you?

Consider this easy example. In one famous company, I heard about how their 100 salespersons brought in 100 million dollars in sales one year. All right, applying the 80-20 Rule then means that 80 million dollars in sales (80%) was sold by the top 20 salespersons (20%). Simple math. Simple.

But wait! Now the New Group of 20 top salespersons who sold 80 million bucks must get the 80-20 Rule treatment, as "all groups" must. That means that $64 million (80% of the 80 million) had to have been sold by the *top* 20% of the New Group, or just four salespersons. Wow! What mighty work was done by those four sales tigers.

But wait! This New-New Group of four *top*-top salespersons, who had sold $64 million must again be subject to the 80-20 Rule. This comes to about $50 million (that is, 80% of the 64 million) in sales had to have been sold by less than *one* salesperson (about 20% of four persons). So now we end up with *less than one salesperson* responsible for 50% of the entire annual company sales! The 80-20 Rule has morphed into the 50-1 Rule. The math was totally honest.

See? The silliness of this "rule" rests with the "...all groups..." part. Otherwise, we have to go with the proof that only a fraction of a salesperson sold all that money by herself.

Maybe it did happen just this way for that company. But how? If true, then there is only one way to explain why the math says that a *fraction* of a person did fully half the heavy selling. Since any company in its right mind could never hire a part-timer with that much skill, clearly this is what happened. This *top*-top-top salesperson was so good that she did all her selling magic by 1:30 PM each day, then took the rest of the day off. Well, why didn't the company hire 100 salespersons like her in the beginning?

But wait....

Stakeholders, Anonymous and Assorted

For a couple decades now we have heard businesses, clubs, nonprofits, communities, governments, etc., tout "stakeholders" as the shiny new objects of their organizations. *Shareholder* is out; *stakeholder* is in. You see, a stakeholder is an *authentic* VIP, a person or group that has a stake in whatever organization about which we are talking.

Why limit VIP status to such mere persons as owners, accountants, chief executives, factory workers, administrative officers and assistants, engineers, and other traditional and dismissible persons? Now lots and lots and lots of other persons, whom we must honor as crucial commercial Stakes in Company X or Charity Y, can speak out with their wise guidance. What a wonderful and humanistic approach to operating organizations! How great a step forward to bringing us all together!

A dyed-blue cynic might notice at this point that calling a person or group a *stakeholder* might end up being sort of like the Wizard of Oz awarding the Cowardly Lion his medal for courage. Everyone being stake-held is happy for the recognition and their role of DESIGNATED IMPORTANCE, whilst the executives or real powers in the organization just quietly "go around" the stakeholders. After all, this could be a good ploy to hold certain noisy groups still, and then pull a switcheroo.

Take heart, though. New stakeholders almost certainly get assigned *authentic* tasks. We will find these days that organizational stakeholders *do* play important parts in their organizations' success, or they expire trying. Consider the actual story of the ill-fated company, Ginron.

Retired engineer Ronald J. Baker formed Ginron to develop and market "grapuronium hydrochloride," an amazing compound he discovered in his lab. This astonishingly flexible product promised to cure the common cold, cement small parts on Navy ships together, and prevent biscuits from burning. Since Engineer Baker hated talking to people, he had to hire a chief of staff to organize his company, and this talented individual became the first stakeholder in Ginron. Thereafter, the company staffed up as lean as possible with additional stakeholders.

A chemist, a physicist, and three manufacturing engineers came on board as the second through sixth stakeholders. At the time, there was a shortage of qualified hydro scientists and grapuronium techs, mainly because no one could spell it. The good salaries offered, however, quickly changed their minds. Ronald's mother was designated the seventh, as an honorarium.

Factory workers to make and package grapuronium hydrochloride couldn't be hired yet, because the product needed to undergo more development in the laboratory, which also needed to be expensively furnished. Remember, though, that mere factory workers do not count as major stakeholders these days.

Adrian Vineswat, the famous environmentalist, was acquired as Stakeholder Eight, to keep the manufacturing process out of legal trouble later.

Jason Ruggemere, the town mayor, was named Stakeholder Nine.

Three important personages in the town became numbers ten, eleven, and twelve. Appointing these three would smooth community relations down the road, particularly when residents begin to identify the odor coming from the plant's exhaust stacks.

By now you can see how stakeholders thirteen through fifty-one were added fairly quickly because of this need, or that, skipping the tedious details. Remember, though, that they were *stakeholders*, therefore important.

The first general meeting of the entire stakeholder grouping could not be held in Ron Baker's lab as it was far too small. A local church offered their space for the event, though Pastor Peterson became Stakeholder Fifty-two by request. His. At the first (and so far only) general stakeholders' meeting, generously described as a "noisy affair," business muddled forward a little slower than expected.

After a few short hours the group meandered toward a consensus, which will be summarized as, "We need cash. Soon." Right-o. Engineer-founder and Stakeholder Number Zero Ron Baker had enormous trouble finding more equity money for their venture. Venture capitalists, "angels," investors, drinking buddies, Mom & Dad—shareholders—had turned him down with such dyspeptic commentary that these sources were dismissed as "having got up on the wrong side of breakfast."

Stakeholder Fifty-three, therefore, had to be the local loan officer at the Bank of Hong Kong and Shakedown. Fortunately, this professional money man injected confidence into the venture by calmly stating, "With a sterling team of stakeholders as gathered here, this plan should be a success, and we shall approve the loan. I'll be here."

Space does not permit making another short story long, so it will be kept short. Although the technical staff fought like tigers with the raw materials to create marketable products from grapuronium hydrochloride, little worked well enough to try selling the stuff.

Trial products turned out instead to burn throats infected with the common cold, turn fittings on Navy ships bright purple, and clump biscuits into an inseparable mass when baked. Except the chief of staff (who made himself more and more absent), most of the stakeholders helped out by giving daily advice to the technical team. Technical teams like it when they get constant nontechnical help. Adrian Vineswat helped by bringing his entire environmental council to the laboratory for one full day, and Pastor Peterson brought cookies.

In fairness, and after the fact, it is likely that Ginron simply ran out of money before they ran out of time. Shareholders, never on the scene at the company because they were considered unimportant from the start, did not join as stakeholders. One by one most of the major stakeholders, however, drifted away from the daily business.

Only Stakeholder Zero, the mostly-absent Stakeholder One, the five technical team stakeholders, and Stakeholder Fifty-two hung around to form the executive committee. The bank loan officer, Stakeholder Fifty-three, now showed up frequently at the executive stakeholder meetings. Calmly as ever, he stood up and solidly said, "I'll be here." Did we mention that as part of the loan package, all stakeholders except one had to co-sign the loan contract?

An unimportant, but interesting fact to note: the name *Enron* had nothing to do with Ron Baker's company name, *Ginron*. It came to Mr. Baker himself one day when one of his buddies slipped him a sloppily handwritten note at the bar, "whatcha drinkin, Ron—gin?" Baker was dyslexic.

Something to think about—the most effective stakeholder in history was the guy that finally put Count Dracula away for good. Certainly he was the most famous.

As part of publicizing this, I had to sign a nondisclosure agreement with other stakeholders.
   -The author/non-cosigning Stakeholder Thirty-one

Department Store Safety Department

N o one reading this has likely known an actual person who slipped on an actual banana peel in a store (fun, though, and every actual boy has tried this at home). Picture some jackass, however, who drops a two-liter lemon soda pop bottle one aisle and thirty seconds ahead of you at the store, making a kind of liquid banana peel. Your shoe hits that invisible poodle-puddle of soda pop, and *bam*! Next thing you know, you are on your back staring at the store's overhead fluorescent light tubes.

You cannot grab the scrawny neck of the sleazy jackass who scurried away quickly in order to avoid blame, but you could stride angrily to the customer service one-way mirror-window place and let them have it. Well, you being a person of quality and good upbringing, would never make a spectacle of yourself (unless this happened in the eyewear department). What you calmly and royally tell them is, "You need a #$&#*@#% ! mop in the #$&#*@#% ! grocery section before any #$&#*@#% ! one else slips on the ...!" But you get the idea. Next thing you know, you hear the Devil speaking for you. The Devil blurts out, "I slipped and fell!"

No, you goofed.

You should have said, "That next person slipping on that soda pop spill, likely a rich lawyer, will sue your buns off." That's only half right, but at least your life will not forever change from having blabbed the first thing out of your whiny mouth about "falling down." Before you can catch your mistake, a very kind and solicitous Department Store Safety Department (DSSD) representative leads you back to the scene of the crime, then back again to the DSSD office after a couple heart-felt tsk-tsk's. All this only lasted three and one-half minutes.

Now the same Devil dumps his nasty details, which will waste your next thirty six and one-half minutes. Once back in the office you sit for five and one-half minutes while the DSSD rep assembles pages of questions and caveats to fill out. If you foolishly brought no book with you, then you get to enjoy piped-in fake Paul Anka music while the pile of forms gets organized for your benefit.

Half the forms you eventually fill in go through the motions of describing the scene of the crime, mostly to let you think the horrible problem will be fixed. It won't, but the forms will soothe you, and will eat up your next nine minutes. The other half of the forms darkly limit the store's liability. Vaguely, these say, "We are hereby and forever absolved of any and all blame, personal or general, for any event occurring in the known or alternative universe, for parties of the first, second and infinite parts, etc." taking up another twenty-two minutes of your day. No wonder. It only takes a few fake-banana-peel capers to make a store go bust. All those forms must be signed on the back as well as the front, in case they lose the front half.

Can you see how admitting to bodily harm, no matter how slight, just dragged you through oodles of valuable time, now wasted? In that 40 minutes you could have easily munched down two burgers and a large side order. Even now things could get worse. The more advanced DSSDs will be sending you an endless string of follow-up questionnaires during the next half year, intended to keep themselves out of jail.

Things could even get *worser* than worse, so do listen, if you are still siding with the store. After filling out the forms, you will be asked—kindly and solicitously—if you need medical assistance.

"NO!!"

Summon all your acting skills to look and sound like General George Patton (or Joan of Arc). Except for compound bone fractures, you must not show any kind of hurt. You are Patton or Arc! Patton or Arc! Say "No!" Sternly. You know all that stuff just said about these forms? Well, if you admit hurt, then you can quadruple your trouble. As Dennis Hopper might say, "Do I have your at-ten-shun?!"

Before I let you go shop, say for some more cookies at this sorry place, let me drill in a cane-wagging truth. Our Founders built this great country of ours on a solid base of danger. Your life is neither simple nor safe, so knock it off with these dainty forms. If cars were meant to be safe, for example, we would have put snow blower engines on them as well as a set of those Tonka Toy tires. Then set the national speed limit at 15 mph.

Instead of going to the DSSD, track down the perp who spilled the soda bottle and bop him on the head with a frozen leg of lamb from the meat cabinet, then go buy that Bo-Peep sheep for tonight's dinner. That scheme worked out really well in an old Alfred Hitchcock TV mystery.

Did you notice that "Department Store Safety Department" also reads logically backwards and still means about the same ugly thing?

The Buffet Rule

T hose salad bar lines, luncheon buffet lines, and coffee lines all seem to accumulate that ten percent of yokels who lollygag around the table after getting their stuff. Very quickly a nice reception or break-time event gets clogged up with dawdling humanity at the front, restless foot-shifting line-waiters at the rear. The standard buffet line is, well, linear. One customer at a time.

Coffee lines create an extra share of this behavior. Picture this common scene at the coffee dispensing table. Three plodding patrons spigot their choice of coffee flavor into their cups, then slowly pour sugar, honey, cinnamon, creamer, one-percent milk, two-percent milk, half-n-half, raw sugar or fake sweetener into same cup, all the while dreamily stirring the cups and solidly blocking all the coffee urns. A few of these good citizens will "help out" by picking up paper napkins to wipe off the counter from the three previous table-blockers. Slowly. This makes for a very tense start for the day. For the average misanthrope, this creates the worst kind of I-told-you-about-people day.

Here's the Buffet Rule: *Scoop your chow, then get your* buff *out of the way*. The shorter version: "Scoop, then *buff* out!"

In fairness, much of this clogged-line problem can be engineered away with inexpensive but astute work-flow changes. Manufacturing people call this "fool-proofing" a process, or designing ways to keep important processes away from self-important fools. The wise buffet line host will have created a "supply side" answer that actually works this time: supply the *condiments* table farther down the line *after* the coffee urns table! Now all these distracted, stirring, pouring, meanderers can doddle-gag as long as they wish around this *secondary* table, leaving the primary coffee urns table open for the serious, briskly moving coffee-cup majority.

Food buffets need more thought. To reengineer a better workflow here, first consider what's called the Salad Plate Predicament. Why, oh why, must we pick up our salad plate before the main stuff plate? The main stuff line usually has what most of us want most, or have paid for. Here we are, going through the downstream *good-stuff* line, banging around a dish with light-weight green stuff and *rolly*, raw vegetables balanced on top. It gets worse if the soup part of the line also sits in front. What to do, what to do? They place salad part first, and the main stuff second, hmmm. Wait! What if we switch that layout? A plan!

"Ho-ho," says the food policeperson, "but then folks will tend to get less of the really-good rolly food, if the Bad Food gets picked first." Ho-ho, indeed. How about this hyper-practical, clever, dish-saving, compromise: do not place any extra plates by the salad part. See? Now the greens can be displayed first, there's no extra plate to bang around through the rest of the line, the food policepersons and the free-choice-persons both get happy, and everyone must be a more careful food stevedore about what goes onto the plate.

Freely admitted: the problem of soup service does not solve itself as easily. Unless. Could not the smart person simply ladle some of the soup over the salad part, and count that as dressing? Technically, that would work. An added benefit to the restaurateur is that almost no one would come back for seconds on the salad. There is no problem too big or too small which doesn't have a ridiculous solution!

Now for the *other* "Buffett Rule," the famous one, which is spelled differently. For readers who do not know the Buffett Rule, named for business tycoon and investor Warren Buffett, this rule basically says that everyone should inherit as much money as Warren B., and then pay it all back in taxes. Or something like that.

Actually, it's not like that at all. Mr. Buffett indeed has shown himself a genius for selecting and operating businesses, and making super-oodles of wealth doing so. There are two smart droplets of advice coming from him over the years which ring nicely. Let's call them both *Buffett Rules*.

The first simply says, after selecting and buying a sound stock, only sell the thing after it drops 10% below its peak. Easy, huh? Name fifteen people you know who can do either of those two steps more than one time in a row. Selecting "sound stocks," if it could be done consistently, would make us all rich, consistently. Forget it. As for the sell 10%-under part? Hah! Most people's egos won't let them. What real man is going to part with his honey-cake stock when it's just dropped? *Real men*, therefore, seldom get rich.

His other rule tells us to swap some good stocks into our portfolio from time to time, and also drop out an equal amount of not-so-good stocks at the same time. If you think the first rule was tough, try doing this baby. *Part with my shares of Pooh-Pooh International just because they're only down fifty percent? Are you nuts? I mean, I've only had them for ten years, and I know they'll come back up. I feel it in my bones!* Well, the bones may feel it, but the poor, suffering wallet has a longer memory. Ditch the Pooh-Pooh (International)! Aren't both of these rules dandy?

Truth be known, maybe Warren Buffet didn't exactly say those things, but he certainly could have. If he had, then no doubt you just heard about one-tenth of one percent of what that extraordinary gent knows.

It's been whispered that Mr. Buffett loves buffets and hates being held up by lines with poor workflow. Such establishments won't see any of *his* dough.

A_ _Book

I sn't Facebook a truly wonderful jump in strategical-tactical marketing technology which has enriched our lives so joyously? So trendy, too. Why, any one of a billion Facebookers can log onto their accounts and go electronically wild with e-socializing. Members can read others' email, post their e-notes, send messages, find out other people's birthdays and send profuse greetings (whether desired or not), put up electronic masks, and exhibition themselves (fictional or otherwise) in a zillion ways too long to list here. Never before has *person-kind* been able to flaunt itself so anonymously. There is much technology in Facebook and even more marketing in it. Also, the National Security Agency (NSA) loves it.

Why does anyone want to spend so much time paddling around in this electronic gruel?

Well, shouldn't this suddenly but surely inspire a "balancing" entrepreneurial idea to burst its way into the sunlight? Misanthropes of all sects certainly will be drawn to a powerful new product, which shall be named "**A _ _ Book**." In the words of that white cat in "Stuart Little," setting up an account in **A _ _ Book** automatically tells the world to, "*Talk to the Butt.*" Clearly, membership makes for an easy no-cost way to make a statement. "Leave me to me, and I don't want to talk about anyone else either. Ever. (By the way, I'm not wearing orange underwear today.)"

Correct full spelling of the new companion website, **A _ _ Book.com**, puts two underlines " _ _" after the "A," because someone ages ago grabbed the all-letters version with the missing S's. Guess by whom, and featuring guess-what on the site? Also, my publisher crankily does not wish to spend jail time, which would be almost as productive as Facebook time. Readers may note that **A _ _ Book.com** exists, but nobody's home; or maybe abandoned without paying taxes.

    A _ _ Book.com has almost no content, because likely users do not want much content. Maybe someday somebody will occupy the site responsibly and flesh it out with some unnecessary design, or something.

    Don't count on it, and don't email me.

Is His Cord Long Enough?

This deals with pop engineering, not biology. If you wanted biology, then switch to that earlier piece, "The Heavy Foot of Carbon Stomps Again" (p. 40).

A guy does have to have a long extension cord—if he wishes to keep his new electric car plugged in while driving around. A one-furlong oval track in the back yard will do (see "Conversions" for a treatment of "furlong," p. 74). Further assuming that Mr. Indy 500 connects fourteen 100-foot 16-gage cords into a fourteen hundred foot string, the driver can screech and corner for about two laps. Then he must turn around and do two laps the other way to avoid an embarrassing and amateurish electrical cord tangle. "He," because very few *she's* would do this silly stuff.

Why is this silly? Clearly, because no one can "peel," "*arrrr-rrr-rrrgharrrr*," or "*harrun-ga-rung-ga-hungahunga*," or make other A.J. Foyt sounds with cars powered like this. So the largest drawback to electric cars is this *Vroom Factor*. Namely, electric cars have none. Inventors who come up with one of these machines that make a real *screech* after the *vroom* (fake, or otherwise) will rake in a bundle.

Let us now follow our new Mr. A.J. Foyt on a short test drive with one of these electrical wonders around, say, a selected Finger Lake in Upstate New York. We have to assume that said car battery has been fully charged, then carried piggyback on a special electric car piggyback truck, and then unloaded at a spot on the north end of a Finger Lake road. At this point, we also assume that the electrical cord has been cut off, because fourteen hundred feet isn't long enough anymore. As he drives southward, A.J. can get to 60 mph quickly because the road pitches downward at a 40-degree angle, and the electric car piggyback truck also gave him a short push on the way off.

What adventure—cornering, screeching, cornering, screeching—what a great way to spend a sunny Saturday Upstate New York afternoon! Too bad about the couple hedgehogs, hawks, squirrels and field mice, plus a few near-extinct species, that got run over because they couldn't hear the electric car coming.

A.J. also forgot about the speed reduction sign at the bottom of this fifteen-mile hill.

For some reason, Finger Lakes towns got built smack at the southern tips of these lakes—the flat part; the part where the steep lakeside cliff roads abruptly level off. Blame the glaciers for the geography, but why on earth did we have to get these brake-burning, sudden-appearing 30 mph limit signs at the point of maximum downhill speed? Maybe the good townsfolk got tired and run down with all these bottom-hill speeders. Who can blame them?

After all this excitement of screeching, cornering, and power braking, our driver decides to celebrate his great gravity ride at a café in the bottom-of-the-hill town. Heck, let the brakes cool off, too. Every one of these towns boasts great little cafés. Just as the dead fauna did not hear the electric car coming at them, though, A.J. doesn't hear enough to take out the key before entering the café. A while later, he discovers that the battery is 'way down. What to do?

Rather than place a humiliating call to his electric car piggyback truck company to come pick him up in town, A.J. decides to drive back out of the town and meet the truck where he got left off earlier. Uphill, this time. Everyone knows the phrase, "Zero to sixty in eight seconds." Now it's "Zero to eight in *sixty* seconds." No screeching this trip, and it takes numerous seconds to do each corner. All goes sort of well, if not slowly, and with many *peeps* and ugly driving gestures from the traffic piling up behind.

Then the battery dies. Sigh. Now he has to call the you-know-what truck. What? Cell phone went dead too? Can't charge up the phone or even connect to the car because....

Now put yourself in A.J.'s driver seat. You have only one self-respecting thing to do. Wait until the traffic clears, turn the electric car around somehow, and then coast back down to town. Spend the night in one of those little hotels in town, and plug in the car for an overnight charge. Tell your friends later this was your Great Plan all along. At least this time on the way downhill, all the many animal species will have warned their buddies that "A.J. is returning."

No-contact Exit Gates

Y ou know those new for-pay parking lot exit gates that take a credit card? You shove your card into the credit card suck-slot, it charges your account, then the arm on the out-gate flaps up. You are on the way without having to make contact with a troublesome human person. These contraptions are fast, dead accurate and none of this, "Good morning, how are you doing today? Have a nice day!"

For those who have not seen these auto-gates, they work like this. You put your parking card into a slot, then you put your credit card into a different slot, and then the gate goes up, and you can get out. Think of an ATM with a second coupon slot. In both cases you have simple inputs and simple outputs: cards go in, and car or cash comes out. Without bothering another person, you are quickly on your way.

Look at it like this—a new style gate is more like a sleekly efficient EZ-Pass machine. The old style parking-attendant gate is more like, say, a bed 'n breakfast. What a delight! No "host" chatting away to "help out" your breakfast, plus you get credit card points *sans* talk. Theoretically, we know these gates, like those EZ-Pass contraptions, could pinpoint your whereabouts. Though, does anyone actually *want* to? Not even the NSA cares, you old self-centered show-off.

Will these gates give us the regulated sameness as checking accounts, restaurants, and Wal-Mart's? Yep, if we have any luck. For those good, caring citizens who crave the human touch, though, there is still room. Fear not: our diverse world also needs energetic and sensitive persons willing to set up awards ceremonies and ski trips.

Have you noticed how persons with bad credit cards never clog up these self-help gates?

Property *Assments*

T his is no typo. When the city assigns a value to one's real property for tax purposes, the noun is correctly spelled "**A—S—S—M—E—N—T**." For persons new to property *assments*, read the following helpful primer.

Property assment Step 1: The first trial which the taxing authorities, sometimes called *assmenters*, use to figure the value of your property is called The Dart Method. A huge aerial map of your general taxing area gets posted to an even huger corkboard. Then several darts are pitched at the map, and the nearest house that was sold to each dart gets averaged to come up with your assment basis. One percent is also added onto this average for each dart used. Step 1's problem is that after many assments get calculated, the map gets ragged, so the addresses, sale prices, and even street names become hard to read. The taxing authority wisely wastes little taxpayer money on extra maps.

Property assment Step 2 comes into play when the Step 1 map hangs down in two floppy, ragged pieces. This next step is called *the Monte Carlo Gambit*. Without getting into the mathematical weeds too deeply with Monte Carlo simulations, let's make this simple. The taxers ("they") could pick a group of properties somewhere around the subject property ("you") by random selection, and average the recent sale prices from those properties. "Random selection" truthfully is a very fair picking method, fairer even than an actual roulette wheel at Monte Carlo. The trouble is, however, that the taxing authority never uses this kind of Monte Carlo method. They go one better. The assment people end up traveling to the real Monte

Carlo (government expense), and pick property prices based on the first 300 numbers that show up on the roulette wheel. Heck, this is almost as random, and twice the fun. Side wagers are allowed.

Property assment Step 3, The Wheel of Fortune Arbiter, is the final say in this whole property assment process. Here, the city buys an old, used wheel from that TV game show. There will almost certainly be a government discount for the purchase. Next, all the wheel wedges get filled with property listings picked by Step 2. Replace that "Bankrupt" wedge with a "get out of jail free" wedged-shaped poster. You can negotiate its use, and you might need it. They spin the wheel four times, then go with the most expensive one that showed up at the top.

Special notice for the case where "you" have to show up for a presentation to the Assment Board ("they"): never, never sit where there are numbers posted on the wall behind you! This rule includes calendars, emergency phone numbers, and graffiti. Such figures could be randomly added onto your eventual property assment total.

Since the taxing authority king will always want their assment agents to come up with *more* money, and the citizenry wants the agents to come up with *less* money, one can easily see how the new title got its spelling. Both king and citizenry want these agents to turn around for a swift kick in the assessment. What a rough way to make a living!

Handicapped Entrances

A ny idea why no business or agency displays a handicapped entrance for misanthropes and geezers? Answer: geezers do not know they are handicapped, and misanthropes do not care.

Take your run-of-the-mill misanthrope. He (she) would simply prefer a regular door, a bit out of the way, where fewer troublesome persons could bother him (her). Recall that misanthropes suffer the disability of not needing to rely on other people constantly. This can take a less serious form such as not having to exchange "good mornings," especially when the other *goodmorningee* wants to talk about it. Knowing that such ideal entrance doors do not exist, and never, never using an actual labeled handicapped entrance, the misanthrope goes through *normal* doors. Thus, misanthropes do not care about special entrances because it is not logical to care about them.

True, geezers do not know they are handicapped, but they tend not to see well. So what, you say? Well, clearly, they do not see the HANDICAPPED ENTRANCE sign, and sometimes end up trudging that special winding two-mile ramp to the door by accident. Standers-by just *tsk-tsk* and shake their heads and chuckle at this mature guy.

Then there are those handicapped parking places. Geezers sometimes get so excited about finding a spot close to the store that they zoom into that extra-wide space, still managing to whack the curbing or the odd newly planted birch sapling. In this case it's all right to tow the old *perp's* car, even though we know he didn't mean to take up the reserved space at all. Heck, they just do not spot the signs.

Those two groups of good souls, never having a handicapped entrance of their own, nevertheless will be the staunchest defenders of the designated handicapped entrance and parking space rules, all the time, everywhere. They both know from experience that citizens with physical difficulties could use those too-rare, but critical time savers in designated public areas. They both also understand *independence*, especially important to their handicapped brethren.

Don't Replace Your Stuff!

D o you know why the country is running out of money? We researched the topic thoroughly and saw that too many people buy too much unnecessary personal replacement stuff. A trifle here, a whim there over the decades, and you can see why our buying got out of control nationally. Several dozen trifles and whims per person, times a zillion population, comes to huge amounts of money spent on unneeded replacements each year. Let's face it—any replacement of any object is going to cost you *something*. We are replacing ourselves out of houses and homes, mostly for silly reasons!

This no-nonsense chat about *personal finance* sounds like *personal responsibility*, only much more expensive. Simply lecturing, "Don't replace stuff until you need to" helps anyone not a whit. It doesn't say *how*.

Well, here's how. Before replacing anything you have, first do this *triage*: label into one of three groups each *hafta'-have* replacement *apple of your eye*. (Experts in languages say, "triage" comes from Latvian for "throwing objects down from the top of a spruce into three separate piles on the ground"). Triage like a pro with these three mental tools: a Type 1 Replacement, a Type 2 Replacement, or a Type 3 Replacement.

Type 1 Don't-Replace Tool: Don't buy a replacement like what you already have, only fresher, or a third spare, none of which you need. "Fresher" means more expensive, and "spare" just boils down to a bald excuse. If you cannot think of five serious reasons why you need to swap out what you already have in your hand (house), then don't buy it! GOOD EXAMPLES:

Perfectly Good Item You Foolishly Want to Replace:	Type 1 "Don't Replace With":
Gel pen & pad	New gel pen & pad
Leather case, strap needs fixing	New leather case
A good book to read	Another book, also unread
Duffle bag, plain	Duffle bag, Army style
Ford Focus ST	New Ford Focus ST
Time out to think	99¢ motivational download

You get the idea.

Food products do not count: dairy, meats and produce; technically here, the old wrinkled stuff is not being replaced. Rather, you are buying something new so you won't kill yourself.

Type 2 Don't-Replace Tool: Don't buy a replacement which offers improvements or tasty features over what you have now, almost certainly not needed. GOOD EXAMPLES:

Perfectly Good Item You Foolishly Want to Replace:	Type 2 "Don't Replace With":
Gel pen & pad	Mont Blanc pen & pad
Leather case, strap needs fixing	New cool laptop case
A good book to read	Kindle, w/more unread books
Duffle bag	Small rolling suitcase
Ford Focus ST	Lexus
Time out to think	Cool motivational CD set

You get the idea.

Type 3 Don't-Replace Tool: Don't buy a replacement unlike what you actually have but which fills the same ridiculous yearning, like, or function. GOOD EXAMPLES:

Perfectly Good Item You Foolishly Want to Replace:	Type 3 "Don't Replace With":
Gel pen & pad	Mont Blanc pen & cool Franklin notebook
Leather case, strap needs fixing	New *laptop* that comes with cool laptop case
A good book to read	Dog
Duffle bag	A very large, cool suitcase to check w/the expensive baggage
Ford Focus ST	A cool single-engine airplane
Time out to think	Dog

You get the idea.

After triaging, the second action you must take: put a pretend miniature geezer on your left shoulder, and a miniature misanthrope on your right shoulder as you triage your possible beloved replacement. The little geezer will just snort "Hah!" as you dither, and the little misanthrope will nag, "So what unimportant person are you trying to impress this time?" This triage, with two little helpers, can talk you out of most any purchase, and will save you oodles of cold cash.

You must also stick to this important rule: never, never attempt a replacement triage, for any reason, when you are standing in a garage sale. This is like don't grocery shop when hungry.

Some objects obviously need no triage, such as:

• A trombone that has been run over by a highway blacktopping roller.

- An electric hand-held food mixer which your kid stuck into wet concrete, and left there for a week.
- A TRS-80 computer.

These objects are called "anchors" by small-boat owners, and are otherwise worth about zero. Do not waste valuable brainpower triaging the trombone if you really want a new one. The little geezer on the left shoulder will remind you how badly you toot the horn, and the little misanthrope will snort about "never making Carnegie Hall," so ignore these sawed-off prudes. Just buy a new horn with the 100% savings you made by *not* buying all that other stuff. You might start your own Don't Replace Club and do the economy some real good.

On the flip side, a thinking person might consider pre-replacing an expensive purchase with a thriftier choice before you buy. Hear that? *Before* you buy! Example: instead of opening your wallet for that overpriced NFL ticket, buy a 12-inch submarine sandwich, loaded, and watch the game on TV. Talk about a *good* Type 3 replacement! And in your heart, you know that any old NFL game will do nicely in place of your blacked-out home game.

You get the idea.

> *Now. Let's get down to business: let's eat....!!!*

THE BUSINESS OF KITCHENS

Yankee Kale

G reens.

If you don't catch onto two of those first three words above, then clearly you must live somewhere north of Virginia. Being of mixed ethnicity myself—southern parents, but growing up near Washington, D.C.—I had believed what I heard as a boy: Yankees don't much like greens. This is not quite true. Most hate them. What a silly, silly prejudice to carry around! One should learn a taste for greens to get better health, widen the menu, and become a first-class snob.

The greens food group includes kale, collards, mustard greens, and other very dark-green and leafy vegetables that won't kill you. You have to cook the daylights out of all of them.

The adjusted northern way to cook greens, let's say kale, goes like this. Grab a large handful of fresh kale, and wash the living pooh out of it. While the kale drains, heat a large pan on the stove and chop up a small handful of onions. Put a couple spoons of oil in the pan and toss in the onions. Whatever oil you can pluck from the pantry will mostly do nicely. Sauté the onions until the kitchen smells good, say, like sautéing onions. "Sauté" is an Upper Dalmatian word which means to fry the food fast, but don't catch on fire.

Now you will see large, ugly center stems running down the center of each leaf. Growing up with the real style cooking, I had to eat these. Remember, you are Yankees, and don't have to put up with that abuse.

Grasp the leaves in a bunch and tear them into three or four smaller bunches. IMPORTANT ASIDE: some books will tell you to roll up the kale and slice into many narrow strips. DO NOT FALL FOR THIS RIDICULOUS WASTE OF TIME! Remember, this is Yankee kale, and you are saving time here, whether you need any more or not.

This may seem odd, but toss the shredded kale into the hot sauté pan. Fry 'em up right along with the onions for a minute, maybe two, tops. Stir 'em, salt 'em, pour a little water into the pan, cover, and turn down the heat. 'Way down. You want to simmer-steam the greens for about 45 minutes. Be aware that all kinds of do-gooders will scold you, preaching shorter cooking times, somewhere around 2-1/2 minutes. Yuk! Kale is a tough old weed and needs to cook long and steady.

Secret Yankee trick: instead of salt and plain water, dissolve a chicken bouillon cube in ½ cup water and use this to simmer the kale. Secret Yankee trick number two: halfway through cooking, stir in a teaspoon of vinegar—this cuts any bitterness and creates balance in the end product. I have no idea what that means, but TV chefs say it all the time.

Uh, oh. What happened to the cornbread? You must serve cornbread with greens of all sorts. No hot cornbread, no greens. Greens without cornbread is uncivilized, it's un-American, it's like a diet. Don't go whipping up a complicated recipe either; just get one of those packaged mixes and follow the directions. By the time you have battered up and poured the cornbread mix into a baking pan, the oven will be hot enough. By rough reckoning, the cornbread will finish baking about the time the kale gets done. What a planner!

Drain the kale, and then plop onto a cutting board. With two sharp knives, slice the cooked kale with scissor-like movements into thin strips. This will feel clumsy at first, but you shall learn quickly. There simply is no other accepted way to cut cooked greens. Do not be a greens-ignoramus! Yankee chef can now place the aromatic fresh kale on the table, along with hot cornbread and butter to your eager guests. People in the know say, "With a big ole' hunka' butta'."

ADDENDUM FOR MALE CHEFS LIVING BELOW MARYLAND: you know *dadgum* well your Momma never cooked greens with bottled oil. Some kind of pork product did the trick. Since we're only talking men here, your best bet comes from cooking up several strips of bacon in the pan first. About five—center cut, thick-sliced, if you can get it. Crisp up the bacon, and set aside. Pour off half the bacon grease (for use with many, many other fattening dishes). Also, don't forget to toss a couple fresh pieces of bacon into the simmer pan. While you wait, polish off those slices of crisped bacon, all five. Be a man!

Some readers may object to my earlier phrase, "...kale, and wash the living pooh out of it." What I am mainly talking about is dirt, sand, tiny rocks, maybe actual or formerly-living objects, and that about covers it. Unless, of course, your kale farmer also is a dairy or sheep farmer....

Dollar Store Kale

"**W**riters' challenges" pester us writers all the time. Some smart-aleck is always posting some see-if-you-can-concoct-this post, challenging other writers to create a poem, essay, short story, play, etc., on a given topic or theme. Luckily, we writers simply do not see most of these floating by to take up our valuable time. The ones we do see, though, tickle our challenge gland into spending all kinds of wasted time on interesting stuff we shouldn't usually think about. Even gold-plated misanthropes feel that idiotic invisible pull of a writers' challenge.

For example, some literary fool recently asked on-screen, "Can you prepare a dinner using dollar store food?" Another fool in another location, let's say an unnamed essayist, then decided to accept the first fool's challenge. He accepted this trivial, non-paying, time-consuming project simply to stop himself from wondering if he could write the fool thing up convincingly. Fool. He did, and here it is in the next paragraphs, this trivial, non-paying, time-consuming but convincing challenge answer.

Yankee Kale, prepared in the way just written about, is the world's Green Standard. A well-done dollar store greens dinner follows closely behind as an award winner. First, a small bait & switch. Apologies. Buy a can of Dollar Tree™ *collards* instead of kale. In the first place, collards makes a little better tasting dish than kale. In the second place, Dollar Tree does not stock canned kale.

If you go to a Super Dollar Tree store, then you will find a chilled and a frozen foods cabinet, just like the big boy grocery stores. The brands may be unrecognizable, and there is only one brand of each delicacy, but one can find a small package of turkey bacon and a six-pack of eggs. Pick up a can of evaporated milk and a package of cornbread mix. Wow, are we ever ready to go!

Open the can of collard greens. You will note that spices come packed into these collards, including a bit of chopped onion. No need to tear raw greens, nor chop up onions as in the "long" version. Peel off at least four strips of turkey bacon, crisp 'em lightly, and dump the greens right on top of the bacon. You will have to add a tad of water to the pan (a tad = a serving spoon which will hold a medium size pebble), and maybe a tablespoon of vinegar. Simmer for 45 minutes. "But," you sputter, flapping your arms around like someone with something important to say, "the greens are already cooked. Why bother!" Because, you greens-ignorant beginner, these dishes always have to be simmered or steamed. It's the law, and it's green.

Meanwhile, you now have time now to whip up a batch of Dollar Tree packaged cornbread. Turn on your toast-n-bake oven, follow the directions on the package, and you will have hot cornbread when the greens get "done." This is why you needed to buy eggs and evaporated milk. You will find that your guests will scoop up every scrap of this meal—collards, bacon, and cornbread even without the butter! If you mistakenly cooked up the whole package of turkey bacon, the guests will inhale these too, leaving you none for the next morning. This is a stupid oversight.

Clearly, do you see the advantages of dollar store greens? There is no washing, shredding, or center-stem cutting of the greens. This is like taking kale from a baby. You need not be as complicated with any of the cooking because the cheap stuff has already been cooked up by some worker at some factory. Such a deal!

Three notes about your dollar store purchases: first, do not read the "fat" content of the evaporated milk. Just buy a can. Second, under no circumstance substitute a package of dollar store biscuit mix for the cornbread. This dreadful stuff mixes up like construction grade drywall patch compound, and tastes worse. When baked, it crumbles into a disgusting pile like week-old PlayDoh™, but could possibly be used to clean up small kitchen spills. Do not serve you or your guests this atrocity. Third, if the store has a stock-out of turkey bacon, you could substitute a package of Genoa salami, or a can of those little Vienna weenies.

The meal, you might suspect, turned out better than the writing challenge itself. After composing this piece, it got submitted to a dark and anonymous writers-challenges den, where the judges took turns pooh-poohing the submissions. They are great misanthropes, too.

Damned Paradoxes

L ife is loaded with things that make no sense. Take this ad in the _____ City daily newspaper a few weeks ago, in the help-wanted section:

"Wanted. Sushi Cook, previous experience: yes."

All right. It doesn't take a Stephen Hawking to figure out that sushi notoriously gets served raw. What's to cook! Further, if only experienced folks need apply, wouldn't that same experienced, intelligent person mention the "raw" glitch right off the bat in the interview? Doing so, however, would mark the candidate as a smart-aleck who would not get the job. Bosses especially do not like to be shown up before they become the boss.

Nothing is left to the restaurant owner but to hire a sushi "cook" who is either a gracious and tactful liar (untrustworthy), a blatant and ungracious ignoramus (an inexperienced, untrustworthy liar), or an illiterate who cannot read. Of the three persons, the illiterate clearly stands out as the logical choice.

There was utterly nothing stated in the ad about reading ability, so there is no moral failing involved in applying for the job. One assumes that a friend of the illiterate applicant read the "sushi" ad to his buddy, so this "D" student could rightfully head down to the restaurant personnel office with his head held high. Nothing fishy here. All might even go well thereafter at the restaurant until the new sushi cook gets a recipe thrust in front of his face....

But wait! We have come to the opposite of what philosophers call a *primary inflated paradox*. Actually, real philosophers *never* say that. That's what I call it, because it has a Latin tang to it. Philosophers wouldn't say that because philosophers don't eat raw fish. Well, that's probably not true either. Socrates, for example, almost certainly did not ever order pizza takeout without anchovies.

Anyway, real philosophers would show that this *whatchamafiddle* paradox is like coming to a stop sign and being required to turn right *and* left. At the same time. But, and aha! We have here a sort of exact opposite setup, though:

Premise 1: a cook who can't read, faced with a
Premise 2: recipe for cooked sushi which
Premise 3: does not—no—*cannot* be cooked.

Therefore, and in conclusion, we have no conclusion.

No harm, no foul. Probably no job.

Selecting Wine

We Americans embarrass ourselves at the tasting table. We say all the wrong phrases, uncomfortably trying to look comfortable. Our every facial wiggle, our movements to and fro, all our small muscular twitches must display more confidence. We Americans must learn competence and grace. We need massive pointers.

First things first. The cork comes first. Otherwise you have nothing much to say (*Gee, that shore looks purty in the bottle*). Remove the cork, and do not bother sniffing it like half the *big boys* do. The other half of the big boys pooh-pooh the practice anyway. The most you should do is say something like, "Look, a cork." Besides, you probably shredded it with a corkscrew, and you would look like a Scythian bumpkin dangling the crumbly pieces.

After sample glasses have been poured, and first sips have been tasted, many pairs of eyeballs, placid as potatoes, are looking at you, awaiting your verdict. This is a verdict on *you*, not the wine. Do not, under any circumstance, take advice from people who use the word "genre" in normal speech. Step confidently up to the pedestal and reflect greatness on yourself with judgments such as:

This tastes barny.
I just remembered to get the car lubed next week.
This hints of burning sugar and plastic.
This one would be great with a wide range of chips.
This smells like a fresh brake job.
Should work well on mosquito bites, inside or out.
Dangy, if this ain't stronger'n Budweiser!

People will be impressed, or at least astonished. Hey, which do you want: to be loved, or to be respected? Now your final purchases must be guided by three important criteria, so think carefully:

1. Decide which wine matches best with a large smoked turkey sandwich. (A solid white or a light red will do equally well.)
2. Feel free to mix corkers with screw tops, and/because:
3. Go for five bucks a bottle, plus case discount.

After the first round of tastings, your friends will still be looking at you for the next step. What comes to mind is that Joan Blondell movie wherein she tries to teach a naïve girlfriend how to bar-talk at a bar. I forgot the name of the movie, but she told her friend how to ask the boyfriend for another drink, something smooth like, "How 'bout another *belt*?" Sophistication like that should not go unrewarded. If you know the name of that movie, though, do not write and tell me. The editor is in cranky humor already.

The reader would be smart to ignore all this important advice above because it is based on faulty pretentions. By all means, when wine-tasting, just display happiness and appreciation. An engineer friend once told me that his only criterion for picking out wine was, "If I likes it, I buys a case."

A Modest Proposal

Yes, I know. Jonathan Swift already had dibs on the title. I have one thing in my favor, however. You see, he is dead.

Recently, exposés have produced stories about questionable new spectacular health regimens. *"Buy this fantabulous 15-day* Nitrogen Carrot Plan *and feel like when you were sixteen!"* Such healthy-life schemes stream endlessly from TV to our brains, all of them looking pretty costly, and all with bad English. Here is one which truly seems like a decent proposal, and fairly low-cost. The name of this new regimen is PERCATOMEN, and you can soon expect its appearance in the advertising media. Each of these existing regimens claims to be The Stuff. Maybe, but these must be objectively judged against sure-fire PERCATOMEN.

The marketing spec sheet for PERCATOMEN touts the product as a nutrient, a disinfectant, and an analgesic. The technical specs: acetaminophen, peroxide, and cat food. Imagine an edible product which cleans its own dish, and leads to a comfortable nap afterwards. The proportions, of course, will remain a manufacturing secret until the patent expires in seventeen years.

Rumor has it that manufacturers of PERCATOMEN worry the public will think the product is a slam on senior citizens. Indeed, this thought came up early in the product development phase. The rumor will fade quickly when the public learns what all we older guys already know. You guessed correctly: acetaminophen does not always work on the exact parts we want it to.

A major plus with PERCATOMEN is its flexibility. Four different varieties will be packaged and sold depending on how many serving dishes the customer wishes to use, how long a nap he desires, and how hungry the household says they are. Labeling will be distinct and clear.

What makes this proposal *modest* is its trusted ingredients and its low cost to the consumer. Further, PERCATOMEN will be posted on eBay, and customers can place bids on various quantities. Do you think any other healthy-life supplement product would dare make such an entrepreneurial offer? Certainly not! It would be wise to stock up before the manufacturer skips town. Remember: "PERCATOMEN has 'CATO' in the middle."

Come to think of it, the Nitrogen Carrot Plan sounds like it could very well give PERCATOMEN a hot race for the profits, even if they don't clean up the grammar in their ad.

More on this used-title business. Now *my* turn has arrived to use the words, then someone else can have the title when I am dead. You see, by then I am too dead to sue. In fact, I won't care *right now* if some other author, nay, if *ten* guilty authors go free to reuse the title I myself have swiped. Heck, I'm one of those guilty ten already.

Manna

We have here a great historical model for a well-fed, boring life. Possibly also very long and boring. Most readers probably know the story of the ancient Israelites escaping from Egypt and pitching headlong into The Promised Land (TPL). Along the way, they were nourished by manna falling from the sky.

Various experts and scholars estimate the amount of time these escapee tribes had to subsist on manna ranging from a short while, to the full forty-plus years of the trek. Especially if we assume that longer time span, the fare must have pretty tedious after, say, three days. Since we also know that the whole forty years' journey was not exactly Moses' most direct route to TPL, one wonders which was worse: the trackless trek, or the trackless meals. The ordeal could be likened to army basic training camp, but without the great menu.

There must have been minor advantages to this manna-meandering lifestyle to make up for all the trouble. For one, it is extremely unlikely that any Israelite grew overly chubby. If we take the book of Exodus at its word, the amount of manna each person could scoop up every day was pretty closely limited, and all that walking in the sand took care of any extra bodily glycogen. For another thing, the amount of distraction on the journey must have been almost zero. The people, however, now had ample time to hone various skills, such as beachcombing and map reading. Except, there likely was no paper-pyrus for sketching.

Someday some other good experts and scholars may be able to answer one of the nagging mysteries of the manna-collecting operation. Namely, did the

Israelites have to wear helmets during the manna-dropping hours? A committee likely was formed to post signs, "Operational Safety Hardhat Area" (OSHA) at designated manna dumps. Since we are told that the manna spoiled very quickly, we now suspect that gatherers had to be dangerously near the OSHA to get their daily scoop in time.

Manna, being at the bottom of a very short food chain, must have gotten old fairly fast, caused in part by lack of desserts. How do we know? For desserts, you need sweeteners. You try simply running down to the nearest Midianite general store and picking up a five-pound sack of sugar. Right! If they had any, which they would not, you would be roundly turned away as a scoundrelly sneaky Egyptian escapee and unwelcome wetback refugee foreigner. Those locals could not have known that your tribes were neither Egyptian nor wet. After all, your people did show up wearing fresh Egyptian duds. Besides, how could they know that it was only the Pharaoh guys who got doused by their clumsy Red Sea caper? These local shopkeepers were decidedly *redseanecks*.

It does not matter. The locals had no sugar. Nobody in the *entire known world* had sugar. The obvious sweetener in those days, of course, was honey. Remember—and this is crucial—the manna refugees had not yet arrived at the Land of Milk and Honey. No cakes, no puddings, no taffy until the tribes arrived at TPL. Even if there were various fruit species occasionally found along the wanderings (a moot historical point by itself), then you still do not have dessert. Manna and figs, manna and dates, manna and melon. These are all *salads*! Was this part left out of Exodus on purpose? Getting to the honey, thus the desserts, was a major incentive for those Israelite tribes to reach TPL. This ploy clearly worked because it only took them a short forty years to cross the border.

There must be a proverb hidden in this somewhere, something like, "When handed a large jar of perishable manna past its expiration, then make manna pie." Oh wait, how do we get the crust? All right then, how about manna rum? Manna schevitz schnapps? Did I say that backwards?

Liver 'n Onions

S ome believe that this dish poisons children. Survivors will tell you about it with much hand gesturing and colorful talk. Some children, however, have a genetic protection against it. These few, however, rarely seem to be the ones who prepare this dish as adults. Odd!

We have heard about the bad effects of eating beef liver. It contains a high level of cholesterol, a 3-oz. serving having about 400 mg of the killer chemical. We know that high cholesterol level in the blood does increase the risk of heart attacks. So does bungee jumping. Also, as they age, cattle's livers tend to build up heavy metals like cadmium, arsenic and lead, which then get passed on to us humans who eat those livers. You *can't* get this from bungee jumping. It seems sensible to simply not eat liver & onions twice every day, and avoid all these problems.

CAUTION! Do know there are two main styles of preparation: tender, or shoe leather. First, a centuries-old belief about eating shoe leather needs to be clarified, especially since it keeps showing up in 18th Century naval combat action novels:

Characteristic	Liver	Shoe Leather
Nutrient content	Good	Good
Chewability	Good	Poor
Availability	Scarce	Good
Preparation time	Medium	Long

Clearly, this table does not do much to settle the matter. Meanwhile, a couple liver 'n onion recipes below will whet the appetite of readers with discriminating palates. Though the internet will usually pop out far more recipes than there are liver fans, these two will be fabulous exceptions:

Liver 'n Onions on the stove:
Ingredients:

1 pound sliced beef liver

Milk, enough to cover the liver in a shallow pan

2 Tbsp butter

1 onion, sliced into rings

1 cup flour

Salt and pepper

How to cook it:
Rinse liver slices and cover with milk in a shallow pan. This gets rid of the bitter taste.

Sauté the onion rings in 1 tablespoons of butter over medium heat until soft. Remove onions and melt remaining butter in the skillet. How goes it so far?

Dump the flour on a plate, then dash in the salt & pepper. Remove the liver from the milk and coat the slices in the flour plate.

Place the coated liver slices in the pan on medium-high heat, and cook until brown on the bottom. Turn and cook on the other side until browned. Add the onions, and reduce heat to medium and cook a little longer. Your call. You will not turn it to shoe leather unless you forget about the stove as you are texting. Dummy.

Luckily, *real men* can find good grilling recipes for liver 'n onions, such as this next one:

Ingredients:
1 onion, sliced or chopped
3 Tbsp (45 mL) balsamic vinegar
1 Tbsp (15 mL) butter, melted
1/2 tsp (2 mL) salt
1/2 tsp (2 mL) pepper
1 tsp (5 mL) mustard, regular or Dijon
1 lb (454 g) thinly sliced beef liver
1 Tbsp (15 mL) vegetable or olive oil

(From *Canadian Living Magazine*, thus the metrics: July 05—thank you!!)

How to cook it:
Place the onions on a small sheet of aluminum foil, then sprinkle on half the balsamic vinegar, butter, salt and pepper. Fold and seal the foil. Place on grill over medium heat; close lid and cook, turning once, about 10 minutes.

Put the remaining vinegar and mustard in a bowl & mix; set aside. Pat liver dry; brush with oil and sprinkle with remaining salt and pepper. Add to greased grill; close lid and grill for 4 minutes. Turn and brush with half of the vinegar mixture; grill, covered, for 2 minutes. Turn and brush with remaining vinegar mixture; grill, covered, until glazed, browned on both sides and slightly pink inside, about 2 minutes. Serve with onions. Wow!

You know, real men can be excused if we drop everything except the "…sprinkle with salt and pepper…." part.

A final note about the liver-leather controversy. Shoe leather clearly matches liver nutritionally, because it comes from the same animal, just different cuts. Although theoretically the two foods do match, the food nazis will pipe up: by the time you boil the leather to edible texture (1-3 days), you have also boiled out all the nutrition molecules. So, grill up a slab of liver instead, follow one of those recipes, and enjoy the afternoon.

I'd Like My Can of Braised Malted Tropical Tuttifruiti

Allegro con brio.
Allegro ma non troppo.
Allegro molto.

Et cetera. They say classical music is essential to the brain, both halves. I love it in spite of all these coded words in a foreign language, probably Middle Devonian, which show up on both the performance programs and the sheet music. Why the heck do intelligent composers say that stuff? Gracious, after all that time composing, scribbling, testing the notes out, and generally fussing for years of a life over their compositions, wouldn't you think they would heartily wish to sell the finished creations (i.e., get rid of them) without that coded stuff? Finally, do they think they are going to impress us? Well, at least they baffle us.

I personally advocate stocking a wide-ranging collection of music in one's personal library. Check out many from the public library for a zero price, but I obviously would never recommend copying the public library stuff and then stashing electronically into your laptop. If anyone should falsely read a pilfering meaning into these paragraphs, then just remember, "This material will be used for personal listening only, never to be re-reproduced and/or sold...." Et cetera.

Such a mixed collection could include rock, blues, jazz, rap, show tunes, country & western selections, as well as classical music (all periods). Such would also be called *eclectic* by those folks who use such phrases as

"Allegro ma non troppo" in complete sentences. I would just call it *fun*.

Real composers would *never* say, "Allegro con brio molto tutti non troppo." You need to know that before trying to use it yourself in a complete sentence.

The Great Kitchen Debate

D o you remember when then-Vice President Richard Nixon traveled to the Soviet Union and had that big debate with Soviet Premier Nikita Khrushchev (Никита Хрущёв, but who's counting)? Of course you don't. In 1959 the United States displayed a model American kitchen at the U.S. Consumer Exhibition in Moscow. One wonders why the Soviet Union at that Cold War time hosted such an event, knowing how their stomachs soured at anything U.S. That is, until finding out that not very many regular Russian citizens were allowed tickets. One came to expect that typical Yes-No kind of thinking in the Soviet Union in those days.

The two superpowers intended this as a cultural exchange, but, of course, with the #1 *mano* of the two most powerful countries in 1959 attending, the meet-up naturally sucked all the oxygen from the pavilion. Imagine these two volatile personages chatting it up amidst all those gleaming modern appliances, circled by a zillion reporters with flashbulb cameras, plus a string of the usual security muscle-men milling about. The next quarter hour of verbal sparring became known as the great Kitchen Debate.

People who hate Richard Nixon will say that the vice president acted stiff and awkward, and those who hate Nikita Khrushchev will say that the man rattled on & on in his usual boorish *poohbah*. Yep, there was a little of both. The truth is, both men were enjoying themselves hugely. Here were two boyish politicians relishing doing what they both did very well: showing off their *one-upman* skills, and each recognizing and respecting the other's natural ability. Both walked away from the afternoon able to plump their chests for their own audiences. This mutual relish could not be more obvious after watching that Kitchen Debate on YouTube, and the reader is encouraged to do so. Nixon touted the fruits of a capitalist economy, and pointed to the huge array of kitchen goods as a small example. Khrushchev rather laughed at these "spoiled fruits" of the capitalist system, and blustered about how Soviet citizens did not need such ridiculous luxuries.

At the time, a large chunk of the world viewed the event, and it, in fact, *was* recorded in color using new U.S. technology, as part of the exhibition. Most people do not know about the unpublicized second half of the Kitchen Debate after the cameras and microphones were turned off, and when most of the strap-hangers had headed off to *happy hour* for white-Russian, black-Russian, and beer-Russian drinks. Sorry, no recipes. Also, no stale jokes about Soviets rushin' to the bar. It was at this point that the rival leaders let down their hair—except Khrushchev didn't have much—and swapped recipes. There were difficulties with translation in both directions, but the exchanges went something like this, jotted down informally by an off-duty journalist.

"All right, here's how to make the world's best meatloaf, you dirty Red Commie cheapskate," says Nixon, with his typical wide-jaw grin. "You mix up some lean ground beef with half again as much ground pork, and a touch of ground veal. That is, if you can scrounge up enough meat in this threadbare burg."

" Oh, we have plenty of meat, you Lyin' Yank!" snorts Khrushchev, "and our steel workers put away more beef in a day than your average puny American softie can gobble in two, you filthy groveling capitalist hog," continues Premier K., hands on chubby hips. "And you Americans are so greedy that you do just that— *gobble* your food. I will now write you out how you make the best Russian vodka borscht, assuming your candy-fed people know the top from the bottom of a beet. Probably not!" (He actually huffed on a quarter hour longer, but the gist is the same.)

"Beets, *schmeets*," the vice president rants on haughtily. "We raise more beets in one state than all of your communes can struggle to dig up, when you have the energy to do so, that is. And our beets are bigger and taste better to boot."

So on and on and on it went, these two grown boys howling it up over food. Sadly, the two recipes have been lost to history, although we have heard that both men took new grocery lists home with them. For the rest of their lives, both men likely enjoyed their new dishes, hugely.

> *Enough politics and food on the plate.*
> *Follow the bouncing history ball as*
> *Poppy now leads you into....*

IN THE UNEVEN KITCHEN OF HISTORY

William Tell's Shotgun

T hat arrow-in-the-apple story has been passed down incorrectly to make the traditional tale less violent. It went like this: the evil ruler Gessler makes William Tell shoot an apple off Tell's kid's head using his crossbow. Mind you, the Swiss were famously good at crossbow stuff, and Herr Tell had qualified as a crack shot. There was a bunch of talking among Tell and Gessler's crowd, and then Tell did split the apple off the kid's head expertly with a bolt (people in the know understand that crossbows do not shoot arrows, but rather *bolts*—shorty arrows, sort of). Then without further talk, Tell whipped around and essentially did the same thing to Gessler's head that he just did with the kid's apple. A bunch more action happened, lots of running and yelling, and then everyone lived happily ever after.

Nothing of the sort happened this way.

To start, William Tell really was a pretty good shot with a crossbow, logging in perfect attendance at his weekend warrior meetings with his local militia, the famous Swiss Chards. Meanwhile, he worked feverishly on his Ph.D., receiving his doctorate in internal combustion gunpowder machinery in record time. His thesis proved to be the first working model of what we would call today, a shotgun. He named this early model the *blunderbûtte*, which resembled the more modern blunderbuss firearm, only noisier and less accurate. In fact, he invented the blunderbûtte to bam north-ambling cows in the south end to get them moving north a little faster. Getting Swiss cows to move quickly up and down mountainsides promised a huge market.

The part about ugly old Gessler making the townspeople bow to his hat on a village pole was true. William Tell and his son did refuse to bow. You can hang your hat on that part too. Now the actual history veers from legend, and we will zoom to the action using the present tense.

Gessler commands Tell & son to bow down, and when they again do not, he indeed does give Tell the chance to save himself and his son if he shoots an apple off his son's head—with the blunderbûtte. The thing looked weird, and might amuse his captive villagers. Gessler was not known for providing humor to much of anybody. "Let me use my crossbow," asks Tell, "I'm a dead shot (so to speak)." "Uh, uh!" snaps Gessler with conviction. "How do I know you won't turn and shoot me also? Dead!" Under the circumstance, his question is reasonable.

"You don't," retorts the proud Tell, as he sneaks a second bolt into his hand. "Besides, the blunderbûtte shoots all over the place."

Gessler flaps his arms around as if he were going to fly, even before paper airplanes had been invented, and howls, "It doesn't matter much how good your aim is here! You know you will hit the apple, you Swiss idiot. Shoot, or William *Tell* becomes dead William *Told*."

Anyway, the story ends when Tell loads the blunderbûtte, stuffs an apple onto the muzzle, and lets'r rip. The contraption fired off and killed mean old

Gessler with a flying baked apple. The phrase "Apple of my eye" started here.

As an important sequel, England liked Dr. Tell's invention, and created the improvement they first named "blunderbutt," But since the English of that era were notoriously poor spellers, those two dots over the "u" cost the printer too much ink, and those ridiculous f's, s's and t's muddle up an already tangled script, we get "blunderbuss" passed down to today, even if the gun is not used any more for serious hunting. Sadly, the 5-meter blunderbuss winter Olympic marksmanship event was earlier canceled because of lack of fast, scrawny German turkeys.

When Hell Froze Over

Something happened to the Atlantic Ocean's *thermocline* one day. *Lorddamercia*! The only people who knew that, oddly, were the scientific ecologists who knew how to pronounce it, and use the gangly word in complete sentences. Those interviewed scientists got to the point quickly, and two and one-half hours later proclaimed, "We think the Atlantic Gulf Stream has stopped." Whoa! Are we going to die by *chillytude*? Break out the camping stoves?

Two sentences will suffice to explain the science: ocean currents normally get formed because colder and denser waters sink, and warmer and "lighter" waters rise, all of which drives ocean currents as the globe turns. Second, saltier water is denser than fresh water. That's it! Physics strikes again!

Take the Atlantic Gulf Stream, for a handy example. Because so much warm water pushes its vigorous way up the northern Atlantic, England and Western Europe get warmer climates than expected at their higher latitudes. Thank you, USA Gulf! Of Mexico. Somewhere way, way up north (Atlantic) the Gulf Stream gets colder (denser) and starts diving down deep. The day the Gulf Stream reportedly stopped, scientists speculated that Arctic ice had melted so much fresh water that the excess up north (Atlantic) caused the saltier water (denser) to dive down much farther south. When a scientist spokesperson *speculates*, he keeps his job; but if he straight-up *says*, he could lose it.

If the Gulf Stream did stop, Europe probably would have a run on sweaters of all fabrics. Some of the *thermoclinian* Ph.D.'s claim that the Atlantic Gulf Stream current really did stop sometime during

American Colonial era, famously causing the great freezes in Europe. Luckily, though, one of the famous personages to actually see, then describe the Atlantic Gulf Stream alive and flowing vigorously was Dr. Joseph Priestly, the accomplished colonial-era British-American scientist.

Another was Dr. Benjamin Franklin *hisself!* Chances are, neither man made all that up. Europe, however, did freeze worse than average during that period. Many canals, rivulets, streams, puddles and chamber pots froze in record numbers during those winters, according to an overwhelming amount of literary and artistic records. From the point of view of a Revolutionary War American looking at Britain, one could say that Hell *did* freeze. Heh.

Further speculation by scientists on the cause of the present Gulf Stream Stop centered on increased pollutants in the Arctic atmosphere, which in turn melted Greenland. This amount of new fresh water certainly could make the northern Atlantic less salty. An important government scientist speculated that Greenland would quickly shrink to the size of a giant Chihuahua, once the ice melted and drained.

What really might have caused such increase in atmospheric pollutants? Polar bears. Sadly, we discovered polar bears in huge numbers participating in weekend SUV drag races. Not only did the racing car exhaust spew carbon dioxide into the Arctic air, but also the bears ate tons of pizza at these regular events. Polar bears do not digest pizza well. Armed scientists have been seen already trekking north to discourage these events in the future.

I say that we are going to find out that the explanation was far more complicated, though, and had nothing to do with bears. Sea life did it! Here's how. When heading northward on the warm Gulf current, Atlantic creatures must swim through the Sargasso Sea. This circulating body of ocean-internal water spawns all kinds of floating seaweeds, providing easy eats for sea creatures lower down the food chain.

Apparently, a new species of seaweed having hallucinogenic properties, *Kelpus maryjaneus*, began drifting through the Sargasso. The first dolphins, whales, barracuda, sea horses, plankton, etc., soon were paddling under the influence of this floating weed as lower food chain sea life ate the weed directly, and one thing led to another, completing the food chain.

These affected lead dolphins, whales, barracuda, sea horses, etc., first drifted around aimlessly with the Sargasso internal flow, then began diving wildly toward the bottom. Since most sea creatures travel in schools, the "D" student creatures bringing up the rear dumbly followed. Such a massive downward movement dragged tons of saltier sea water (denser) with the creatures.

At this point, you need to know the normal global path of the Gulf Stream. No less an authority than the late Stephen H. Schneider (*Global Warming*, Sierra Club Books, San Francisco, 1989, p. 52) traces the ocean current's path after dipping down in the North Atlantic. It spreads out, Schneider explains, into the deep South Atlantic and under the Indian Ocean, into the Pacific, up at the Aleutian Islands (Alaska), back down over Indonesia and Australia, and returning through the Indian and South Atlantic Oceans by surface to the "starting" point. Dr. Schneider, though, never figured the kink in the flow caused by the potent, but natural seaweed mishap. Not his fault.

By now the massive amounts of sea life, along with very salty, dense sea water, headed around Africa for the Indian Ocean leg of the trip. Almost all these good creatures were too stoned to make the left turn shortcut through the Mediterranean and the Suez Canal. By the time the vast majority of sea life crashed from their Sargasso high, they also crashed smack into the Maldives, that famous island chain nation in the Indian Ocean.

The Maldivians thought they had problems already, with their islands purportedly sinking. Dr. Schneider told them so. Now they had fifteen million tons of cranky sea thugs shaking the volcanic foundations of their island nation. That's every second. Worse, the now-crashed sea things were in such a foul humor that each one bammed into the islands a second time for spite.

The Maldivian Secretary of the Interior, who was also their Secretary of the Exterior, suspected something fishy was happening to his homeland's geology in the first couple days. Thereafter, the earthen deterioration of their many islands proceeded quickly, so this good official headed up a large emigration to Saudi Arabia and Oman. Very soon, 95% of the nation had relocated. Thereupon, the Maldivians, seeing that the prevailing Saudi and Omani wages were eight and one-half percent higher than their own previous homeland average, stayed.

As luck would have it, Saudi Arabia and Oman experienced a boom in tourism to the now-smaller Maldives, thus badly needed the former occupants as guides and divers. Now, some of the world believes that "Maldives" come from the French for "bad divers." It didn't, but this was an error in any case. The ocean skills of these people are unsurpassed. It will likely happen that these Maldivian expats will soon shorten their official name simply to "'Deeves."

As for the ecological disaster just described, England and Western Europe actually noticed little change in temperatures these days, because branches of the Gulf Stream still squiggled around the Sargasso Sea. Also, hippie-looking boat crews by the hundreds now have been launching daily from all North American east coast ports, reported to be collecting the new Sargasso seaweed for useful medical experiments. This new massing scientific navy has punched all kinds of holes in the Sargasso blockage. But *all hell could have broken loose,* and the whole shebang *could* have frozen over.

I realize that faults can be found with this piece. The major one, which I will correct for the next edition, came from choosing a preposition to end the title with. The new title next time will, therefore, be: "Over When Hell Froze."

The War of 1812

Y eah, there was one. Like Korea, this "other war" people either do not think about much, or do not know it happened. There was that Johnny Horton song about the final battle of the War of 1812, though he got the "1814... took a little trip..." wrong, but who's counting a few days into 1815? Oh, also there was that movie about the war, where Andrew Jackson played Charlton Heston, and Jean Lafitte played the hero-pirate Yul Brenner—with hair! Both song and movie go a long way back.

The thing is, after the War of 1812, the United States and Britain never again seriously scuffled over major issues, and grew into fast allies in World Wars I and II. This alone should make us respect anew this conflict, which gets kind of tucked out of sight between the Revolutionary War and the Civil War.

Another war that got an all-numbers name would be the Seven Years' War. This is the French and Indian War to Americans, the English and Indian War to the French, and the Assorted White Men's War to the Indians. Like those much earlier Hundred Years' War and the Thirty Years' War, Europeans cleverly did not say *which* seven, *which* hundred or thirty years they were talking about.

In the long run that backfired, because people do not take the time to look up all those events these days. Too confusing. Our War of 1812 said *exactly* when it happened. Luckily no one dared name it the Two and a Half Years' War. Aren't we practical!

Attila the Honey

History has been unkind to our women. Not a very large number of famous-woman stories from older times have been passed down to us. Let us straighten up this shameful situation with a short list and reminder of some real historical babes.

Ruth (Bible). She comes down to us as likely the oldest model of someone whose deeds promote the well-being of others close to her. In this case, her mother-in-law (Naomi) was understandably in a very bad mental way after her husband and sons' deaths. Ruth was not legally obligated to go with Naomi, but she did, sensing the very great psychological needs of her mother-in-law. She later took work "gleaning the grain fields" to get income for the family group, and that all sounds cute and tame today. Imagine a young woman taking work, say, with those early railroad gangs in America as a coal cinder picker-upper in front of the trains inching behind the cursing and shouting track-laying teams. Or how about her taking a job as a nighttime street security patroller in the middle of Los Angeles. Alone. Unarmed. You get the idea. She did risky stuff for the family to survive. She also gets credit for becoming King David's great-grandmother. What a honey!

Esther (also Bible). Esther's story, with a tangled childhood, twirls and winds about somewhat more complicated than Ruth's. She didn't have to worry about dealing with rough old cornfield-gleaning gangs, but she had other problems: rough old kings. In this case, the main thug was King Xerxes. "Xerxes" in Greek (for a *Persian* king, no less) means "Berserker Light of the Jerks," so you see how he gets *his* name, and *you* get a hint of this nutball's attitudes. After a hugely abnormal number of events, adventures and outright dangerous situations, Xerxes dumps his current spouse and substitutes Esther (eventually). Esther parlays this good fortune into saving the regional Jews from harassment and executions by Xerxes's crazy bunch. For this fury of activity, she is credited and remembered with the Jewish annual feast of Purim. What a honey!

Boudicca. This first century AD warrior queen almost led the complete rout and ouster of Roman armies stationed in Britain who had invaded and occupied her island decades earlier. She became queen by default when her king-husband died unexpectedly, and after the Romans treated her and her tribes roughly. The Roman military mostly looked at her barbarian army with disgust and disdain, but these early united Britons swiftly overran several Roman towns and a large military unit, to the disbelief of all. In the end, hubris got the better of the Britons, and they were badly outgeneraled by the Roman Governor-General Paulinus, with devastating after-effects for the native Britons. Apparently Paulinus repressed the country so severely that a horrified Emperor Nero recalled him to Rome. Imagine, being fired by Nero, and because of a *girl*! They say that Queen Victoria should have used Boudicca's name as her namesake. Maybe. If you travel to London, you will see a statue of Boudicca. Likely she was a six-footer with a rough, commanding voice, so said by chroniclers at the time. What a honey!

Eleanor of Aquitaine. She was probably the only A.D.D. personage named here. Some people are born to be behaviorally all over the place, and Eleanor probably started the practice, unless you include Julius

Caesar. We won't, because this is a babes-only section. Eleanor wed Louis VII of France, then promptly whisked herself off on the Second Crusade with her new husband. Neither the Crusade nor the marriage worked out. Apparently devout Louis had eyes for a Jerusalem pilgrimage, and Eleanor had eyes for everything and almost everyone else. She, being clearly cleverer than he, found a way to get a Church divorce after several persistent tries. Thereafter, she was free to wed the future Henry II of England. In spite of the fact that Henry later on imprisoned her for a decade for being, well, Eleanor, the two of them were clearly the ultimate power couple of the day. He predeceased her, and two of their eight children became kings later on: Richard ("Lionheart"; the one Robin Hood traveled with in the movies), and John (the cranky *Magna Carta* guy). She is credited with later smoothing the many discords among her royal brood. What a honey!

Joan of Arc: Young Joan worked far harder at conquering than general history books credit her. She didn't merely rise up one day, find a small spare suit of armor lying around, and then lead a French army to whup a superior English force all in one quick rise-up. Whatever vision or string of visions she may have had about being commanded to rise up and smite the English, it was only a couple years later that she could be found crashing her way across northern France, demanding to meet kings and commanders to force them by turns to fiercer resistance against the English, those evil foreigners. Why, those interlopers could never even pronounce "foreigner" in good French. She campaigned with various French forces for about a year before being captured. This military period was spent pushing, cajoling, shaming, leading, all of which was hard, risky work. Extremely risky work. A reluctant French military didn't warm quickly to being led by a *girl*, much less one whom people might blame as a crazy heretic. She got herself wounded by arrows and crossbow bolts several times. Eventually captured, tried for heresy, and executed by the English, then reinstated a decade later, then eventually canonized, she remains probably the most important historical hero in France today. What a honey!

Pocahontas: We have in her probably the first famous "mother of two nations." Oh, forget that interesting, but likely untrue story of saving settler-soldier John Smith from a head thumping by placing her head over his on the head-bopping block. Maybe this preteen girl did do such a deed, though John Smith gained fame using his own extraordinary exploring skills through the strange and dangerous new land of Virginia. Pocahontas proved *her* extraordinary ability to explore her way through that strange new world of white men arriving from all over the place. Later marrying the accomplished colonist John Rolfe, she used her intelligence and flexibility to become accomplished and respected herself by the English speaking world. Her son, Thomas Rolfe, became one of the "First Families of Virginia." As long as she was alive, she served as a true *mediator extraordinaire* between two very different cultures. More than once she saved the early Jamestown colonists from starvation (in their new land of plenty) by bringing food to bridge them over hard times. What a honey!

Everybody knows that Attila's wife never went by "Mrs. Attila." It was "Attila the Honey" to anyone prizing their life. So, which of these women would fill her mighty shoes? Matter of fact, except for rich

Eleanor, none probably had a large shoe closet. Including Attila the Honey. Except for young Joan, none required shoes for their talents to blaze through. Let's just correctly call these Major Honeys. Why not call all women Major Honeys also!

A stern note to favorite readers: hopefully, I will not get a quarter-zillion ugly emails telling me that so-and-so should have been on my babes' list. Let me say this: you are right. Before you even send me that email, or even if you do not send it, or even if you had not thought about so yet, you are right. Pre-*mea-culpa*. You are *all* my favorite readers.

A Childhood Story

There was once a "simpleton" farmer who brought the king a beautiful horse as a gift, and asked for a *beating* as a reward. There is more to the middle of this story, of course, and it can be easily summarized.

See, the farmer had to pass through the usual two evil royal advisors before presenting the horse to His Highness. Each of these two greedy, evil bozos told our good farmer that he had to hand over half the farmer's reward from the king on the way *out* the castle, else he would not get *in* the castle. Two halves of the reward subtracted from the whole reward added up to about zero left for the farmer. Therefore, and in conclusion, when the king asked the good farmer what he wished for a reward, and with the two bozos whispering "jewels and cash" in the farmer's ear, our hero asked for a beating instead! Each bozo adviser was thus entitled to one-half beating. The king, being of good nature and humor, sent the royal advisors out for a *half* thrashing each and RE-rewarded the farmer with good stuff, chortling all the while. The exact RE-reward likely involved a hearty dinner and a position as Chief Kingdom Bureaucrat.

A great story, because as a kid, you're rooting for the simpleton and against the bullies. Still, problems lingered. You know what nags a child's mind about this tale? When did this supposed simpleton's brain switch tracks from being a guileless and—all right, a simple dummy—to an Einstein-like head complex enough to make up a three-level risky prank like that beating-for-reward thing? Why, if we could figure out how this brain switch happened, we might prevent most accidents from getting elected to Congress.

Further, how came the king to hiring two nitwits like that for advisors? These two stupids did not even bother to coordinate their racket with each other, thereby stealing a little less from each visitor and making up for it on volume over the years. Surely the king would recognize that the inflow of good fortune and good people to the castle had stopped at exactly one visitor—the very first one. Reputations, after all, traveled fast even back in castle days. The best explanation came from a younger mind, who said, "It wouldn't be a childhood story!"

OK, but what the heck is *half* a beating, anyway?

Earth Day

A celebration of Earth Day started out as a huge celebration of what—earth? That means throwing a party for *dirt*? Let us now look to the great Earth Charter for some good information and answers.

Never heard of this Earth Charter? The same gent who invented Earth Day decided to keep his hand in the compost pile by inventing the Earth Charter a decade later. Summary: he wrote up the Charter with four Pillars and sixteen Principles—four Principles per Pillar for balance, we suppose, or merely to limit the counting to only one hand. All of these basically declare the importance of *everybody* to *everything*, both past and future, and *vice versa*.

Tending to all sixteen of these Principles would make another long chapter, thus tempting this book's editor to burn the manuscript in a huff. He grudgingly agreed, though, that a short summary of the Pillars alone would add to the reader's understanding of Earth Day, and would not be too large a waste of time and ink. I promise.

Pillar The First: Respect and love and understand all societies, species, and peaceful intentions; and "secure Earth's bounty and beauty for present and future generations." Now who the heck can argue with respecting and loving all those worthy societies, species and intentions? Who shall be the nature-wrecker who steps on innocent slugs?

The second half of this Pillar #1, though, should make everyone scratch their puzzled heads. How is one to know exactly what needs to be preserved, and in what condition? If, for example, during the next 200 hours a species or earthen object breaks or extincts itself, do we issue a do-over certificate to, for—what? For re-creation at some future time when technologies catch up? This ought to create oodles of spectacular jobs, the titles for which also have to be made up.

For the moment, here is a fabulous answer to preserving what we have right now for future generations: pickle one of each species or object, or both. Better make that two of each in the biology grouping. Store them in the Smithsonian basement. This sounds much less dangerous than taking DNA cheek swabs from some of the larger animals in the cat family.

We need not concern ourselves with the most fundamental of all Earth Day substances: earth. *Dirt*. Dirt will preserve all by itself, and they say it's cheap.

Pillar The Second: Besides protecting & restoring Earth's ecological systems already mentioned, we have to use the "precautionary approach" when we are not sure about what we are doing. Does this include a precaution about restoring various dinosaur-like animals from a few tens of million years ago? Oh wait; there was already a movie about that. Not many folks would like the idea of being buzzed by pterodactyls at a family picnic. This "precautionary approach" thing really means, in English, when you don't know what you are doing, then don't do it. Since we never really know what we are doing, then we never have to do anything. This makes our obligations simpler, and we can settle for universal pickling, as in Pillar #I.

Pillar The Third: Get rid of all poverty, make everything and everybody equal, and brook no discrimination, except for special attention given to the rights of indigenous peoples. Sounds good, sign me up!

This certainly means that everybody on Earth gets to vote on who is poor, but won't be, and who is not getting their share of world equity, and how all this gets rewarded or rearranged hour by hour, and who the "indigenous peoples" are, and if they get to be part of the chooser class, but since there's all equity everywhere (except when there isn't), the indigenous-class group would have to keep shifting around in order to share everything.... Gads! We can sort out the details later.

Pillar The Fourth: This pillar seemed to push a bunch of ideas together, probably in a rush to a publishing deadline. Writers know how horrible these can be. Two ideas stand out, though, probably to wheedle in the main ideas from the Charter Inventor. The first idea strongly advocates *participation in, and decisions for all Earth matters by everyone, all the time.* Every person would likely have to be issued an electronic vote-box to pull off this ambitious goal. Mandatory Twitter?

The second Pillar #4 idea orders that *all living beings be treated with respect and consideration.* Would this include *Yersinia pestis*, the bubonic plague bacterium? After refinement and careful thought, though, the second idea blends with the first. Let us see if we understand this big, Blended Idea: every adult must show total *respect,* both by voting once a day on Earthy kinds of proposals, and also by not harming living things, except for bacteria or ugly weeds. No spraying slugs, unless they exceed four, and are heading for the lettuce garden.

All the Charter stuff above involves theoretical ideas. We turn at last to a couple *practical* good deeds which we can do on Earth Day. The first tends to the matter of careless gasoline spills left in the ground. Make sure all shut-down gas stations get signs jammed into the vacant lot saying, "Closed. Condamned. Clean up, or die!" These could also double for use the other 364 days in front of teenagers' bedrooms. Maybe not the "die" part. Maybe not the "condamned" part either.

A second practical deed aims to cut down on carbon dioxide put into the atmosphere. Stop breathing for 40 seconds. That's "one rep," as they say at the gym. Perform 40 reps before you quit for the day. Doing this will save zillions of tons of carbon dioxide, as long as no one cheats and breathes deeply afterwards to make up for it.

Of course, if, among the participants, some geezers expire from the good deed, the increased methane released into the atmosphere from their dead bodies will undo all the good they just accomplished. Since our motto is "Decreased Before Deceased," we may celebrate his decreased carbon dioxide by itself, and see if the old coot left a six-pack in the trunk of his car. No belching *Cee-Oh-Two*, please.

Before the year 2022, someone should think about setting up and celebrating Mars Day, because that's where we may have to go live if the Earth Day Charter goes into effect. This would be a great *precautionary approach*, no?

A famous scientist notes, "wealthier is healthier" when referring to environmentally better-off countries. Would it not be easier than doing all these good practical deeds, and all this chartering, to simply push for all zillion persons on earth to get richer?

Escape from the GULAG

T his strange tale began with an odd delivery into the side door of a local urgent care medical center (reliably told below by Poppy himself.)

"A thirtyish delivery man was wheeling a large package from his UPS truck, and into the side door of that center. The cart he pushed carried a large, floppy package, and looked more like one of those brass wheely things on which you move suitcases through a nice hotel.

"I shook my head with only the wispiest of wonder and drove on to other morning errands. An hour later in front of a grocery store, a seventyish man got out of a van displaying the logo from that same urgent care center I had driven by earlier. This man walked jauntily, with an air of confident masculinity. Something looked familiar about him, but my brain was unable to connect the wires.

"Later, from the evening news I pieced together the remarkable string of events which must have happened, though the news people had not caught up with it yet. The story headline ran something like, 'Today a vehicle from the _____ Urgent Care Center, Inc., was stolen by an *unknown perpetrator*. Police are on the lookout for a probable male driver, now on the run, description not clear. An employee of the center was also found bound and gagged in the center's loading dock area. A further mystery exists in that an old, unregistered UPS truck was found abandoned in the parking lot. Anyone seeing ....., etc.'

"All brain molecules now firing, I realized what had looked familiar about the older man at the grocery store that afternoon. His shirt was almost certainly the same as the delivery man's. In fact, his face looked like an older version of the delivery man's!

"Clearly, here is what happened. The younger man had been carting his crazy or troublesome uncle to the urgent care center in a found UPS truck for *processing*. This crazy geezer, however, also turned out to be quite physically fit, and held a simpler view about 'being processed.' His nephew worked at the center, thus would not have aroused suspicion by wandering around the building's loading area.

"Although the older man had earlier somehow been surprised and jumped, tied up, bundled, and driven into the urgent care center, the tables turned after his being un-bundled in the loading dock. Very quickly this older man overpowered his unfortunate kidnapper, tied him up, swiped his shirt, then taped this upstart's mouth. The *processing* step was skipped.

"Pulling a huge bundle of keys from the younger man's pocket, the older man quickly walked to the parking area and picked one of the center's vans for his getaway. Whistling 'No More Cane on the Brazos,' he soon found the right ignition key, and away he sped.

"Clearly, this actual drama must have unfolded just like that.

"We do not know what the old guy bought at the grocery store, but let's say he picked up a six-pack and a submarine sandwich, then drove toward his home. Not being entirely crazy, he stopped a mile from his house, and before abandoning the van, wiped down the steering wheel, gear shift, key chain, and door handle. Whistling 'Rhino in the Pantry,' he sauntered home for a tasty meal. Free again.

"You think the police would be after the old gent, don't you? Not yet. The center's van would be found later, with the younger man's keys dangling in the ignition.

"A possible follow-on story might go like this: The poor young employee had been surprised and tied up in the loading dock where he worked by ..... an unknown assailant! Obviously, the perp would have abandoned his stolen UPS truck in order to swipe the care center company's van for his escape, so far for reasons unknown.

"Assailant's description? 'Don't know,' pleads the young apparent victim, 'I got snuck up on and knocked cold from the back. Next thing I knew, I was being woke up by one of the doctors at my center.'

"Will the police figure this all out? Will the reporters ever catch up with the actual story? Should I say something?

"If the young relative ever, ever dared show up later at the old man's house, even wearing a flak jacket, he still would be almost entirely vulnerable to the old man's current pistol license. The old man, of course, would tell the police that he was, 'Sure he was warding off an *unknown assailant*.'"

The Most Unluckiest Geezer in History

A long time ago in a country in the center of an unimportant continent, there was an important kingdom ruled by the famous King Chipŏziy. This name was too hard to say, even for the good folk who spoke that language, so he was simply called King Chip. For decades, King Chip ruled with great wisdom and cleverness, increasing the wealth and prestige of his country.

In recent years, though, he began acting strangely as he aged. One of his baffling decrees ordered a large blowtorch factory to duke it out with the national ice-cream factory. The ice cream works could use catapults, and the blowtorch manufactury could use their Big Bertha fire launcher, a truly wondrous tool that could singe a bullfrog's butt at twenty-five yards. A huge crowd gathered to watch a sloppy, combative afternoon, at the end of which the blowtorch works were fatally clogged, and the ice cream factory was a pile of gooey cinders, and creditors were demanding payments. What a mess! Everyone guffawed all afternoon, along with King Chip. What fun everyone had! For one day.

Since a quarter of the kingdom were employed by the blowtorch company, and another quarter at the ice creamery, economic depression struck hard and immediately. Grumbling about King Chip was rampant, all the way to its borders.

The Old King Chip also began making diplomatic blunders as well. During an important state dinner one evening, when the visiting prime minister had been talking glowingly about the good relations between the two countries, the old king burst out with a string of uncomplimentary noises. King Chip escaped from either explaining or excusing himself, by promptly falling asleep, loudly. He compounded his gaffe, and confounded his own ministers the next morning at a joint military conference. There he demonstrated to all what he had done the evening before with a detailed reenactment, complete with excellent imitation sound effects, guffawing hugely all the while. Old King Chip had become a kingdom liability.

His court whispered that during a recent morning stroll he had stepped juicily into a large wayside pile of canine poop, and said nothing. In his prime, the then-*Prince* Chip would have gone into a monster respiratory windup, inhaling for thirty seconds before cutting loose with a long, burning string of ugly words, and naming all the things he was going to do with the kingdom's dogs. But this time he had simply inspected his boot, then guffawed loudly. Something badly wrong had snapped in His Majesty's mind.

The king's son, Young Prince Chipőziy II (royals often lack imagination), now a handsome and intelligent young man, had been showing an increasing knack and skill at governing various aspects of the kingdom. Clearly, he would be a better choice to run things, the sooner the better. The major ministers pondered how to get the reins swapped to Chip, Jr. The kingdom was a constitutional monarchy, with much power given to both constitution and monarch. They couldn't simply impound the old man, and the constitution did not allow abdications. Joint rulership was strictly prohibited.

The constitution only allowed succession by death of the reigning monarch. That night, the Royal Archivist pored through the country's constitution to find some means, some clause that could safely usher in the Young Prince Chip II in place of his father. The answer opened up to this talented bureaucrat in a flash.

Feverishly the next day the Royal Archivist and the Royal Scheduler set up a royal visit to the neighboring country's capital, an important city near their common border. The constitution was quite specific about what must happen when the king traveled abroad:

Article IX, Sect. 3-2.7 reads in part: "...and when the King visits foreign countries, ceremonial preparations will be paramount, making certain that his trumpeter shall be sent ahead, after which the King's arrival shall be announced...." The ministers finalized their plans and guided King Chip to a small room on the way to his chambers to prepare for the planned trip. There he passed the royal guardsman, who was armed with a large battleax. The guard had his specific instructions.

"Say, you got an ax to grind with me, guardie-wardie?" guffawed the old king loudly.

Ka-chunk!

Following their constitution to the letter, the two ministers immediately sent the royal trumpeter (who had been dispatched to the foreign city the day before) a head. The king's. Clearly, everything was now in order. The country needed a new king, the royal trumpeter had been sent a head, and the old king was certainly dead. Both top and bottom halves.

Figuring that the personal danger to himself was slight at this time, the Royal Scheduler, as required, then announced to the court, "Well, that's a block off the Old Chip."

Mr. Bates

D o not call *adventure* fun while it happens. It may even risk killing you for real. Someone unknown to me said that. I wish I had thought of it first.

When your mother packed you off to school, the first day of your school life, to stand at the bus stop 'way, 'way away, this first real adventure should have been scary. The vast 200-foot distance from her front door to the bus stop did not seem scary, though, just different. Dressed up like an idiotic six-year-old going to the first day of school, ever, you were supposed to wave down the bus with a ridiculous arm motion, being careful not to do so to a Greyhound.

The school bus ride should have been scary too. Sure, the other youngsters were talking loudly in an Older Kid chatter, but you didn't need to understand much anyway. The scary part clearly had to be what waited at the other end of the first-day bus trip. The bus ride wasn't especially so.

The Great Principle of adventure says that while you are adventuring, your head thinks only about surviving the next three minutes. No time for being scared. Another Great Principal was Mrs. Simms, head of the elementary school. She knew she needed to be there for all of you, literally, even before that silly phrase was coined, for the disastrous *homeward* bus rides.

When you go *to* school, there is one bus going to one place. When you go *home*, there are many buses going to many places. How do you manage this when you are six years old? The school part of the day oddly came and went without memory. All right, I will now put *me* where I had been putting *you*. I met Mr. Bates on the homeward bus trip. He was a geezer of importance. He drove school bus number 6, and I had no idea what number I should take. He and his bus looked as good as any choice, and maybe I should have thought that the driver and bus number on the way in would be the same on the way out. Details, details. Onto number 6 bus I climbed.

The other kids were chattering a loud Big Kid kind of talk, like the morning, but the road and the scenery did not look anything like the way back to my house. Gradually, the kid crowd in the bus dwindled, as did the chatter. There was I, alone, two-thirds the way to the back of the bus, not chattering.

Poor Mr. Bates. What to do with this nonspeaking sawed-off leftover who had no idea how to explain in what part of the universe he had to be dumped off? But, not-so-poor Mr. Bates. This gentleman, and he truly was, had been through this before with kids dumb enough to be blunt objects. Back to school he drove, for sure a goodly amount of time out of his way, and into the school parking lot.

He didn't say much, but took me by the hand into the schoolyard, where Mrs. Simms waited for gumball six year olds who had earlier that day waited 200 feet from their mothers' front doors for the first school bus that morning, and who refused to wave the bus down, and hadn't had the sense to catch even the remotely right bus home. Those were the days when an older, kind man could take a strange little boy by the hand to safety.

Well, what does one do next with a little boy, too shy to speak his name, and whom one wishes would disappear so one could finally go home? Mrs. Simms was *never* ruffled, so she flipped through a notebook, speaking each new kid's name listed there, slowly asking, "Are you James?"

No.

"Are you Bill?"

No.

"Are you Peter?"

No.

Honestly! *I* would have smacked me upside the head if I were my own large, nearby twin.

Mrs. Simms must have been through this one, at least three times before in her long principal's career. She was really old, probably about thirty-seven or thirty-eight. After eventually and patiently running across my name (the little idiot in front of her finally reacted "Yes"), Mrs. Simms had someone call my parents. Next thing I remember, my father showed up, not especially distressed, and we both went home. I hope he thanked Mrs. Simms and Mr. Bates.

My father, Mrs. Simms, and Mr. Bates all did the right thing by not showing alarm. After all, this was a real first adventure, and adventures may not be enjoyable during the action. Afterward, though, we recall the adventure parts, and thank a hundred times those good people who made sure that we survived.

Geezer Einstein

Was Einstein a geezer? Was Einstein a misanthrope? We shall explore both. First, though, "Einstein" brings up two head images immediately: *smarts*, and *hair*.

I recall back when The Great Man died in 1955, the kids in my Sunday school class were talking about how *Frankenstein* had died that week. Not surprisingly, they all wanted to talk about it—Frankenstein, that is. That's even after being explained that the famous scientist was not that big guy with the bolt through the neck.

Did young Albert's hair actually bother anybody at the time? His distant cousins reportedly asked on many occasions, "Hey Ein," as relatives called him, "you ever think about getting a shorter *do*?" He must have said "No!" because his *do* stayed more or less unchanged over the next century. Stubborn guy.

Researchers of tactical-sociological science claim they have pinpointed the exact time when Dr. Einstein turned geezer. This happened, these experts explain, when he famously announced his "cosmological constant" excuse. For the lay-person, the story goes something like this. Middle aged Albert had been chasing a cosmetologist named Konstanz Sternlicht. He said she "had big insights he needed." Indeed. What a bumpkin. This incident is widely misunderstood as his Big Mistake. Not really. The time Dr. Einstein turned geezer was when he realized much later that his "cosmological constant" (not the girlfriend) turned out to be a good idea, sort of. Geezers have to earn their label, and the good Doctor realized that his theory of relativity had a sizable black hole in it. Earlier he thought he had an easy way to cover it up, later realized that his cover-up was dumb, retracted contritely, and then took little credit when it looked as if he might have been right all along. Sort of.

Still, this man seems to be the kind of guy you could go out for a pint and a *brat* at the local *stube*. Occasionally. People probably think, from the photos we have of Einstein, that he was an intense loner, and therefore a misanthrope. Not usually, however. He apparently not only enjoyed the company of colleagues but also frequently needed their input. That is unless they were troublesome, or clogged his thinking tubes. Certainly he had confidence in his own ability, but don't be fooled. Too many times he showed how much he really needed his colleagues, and he could be extremely generous in his endorsements.

These same oddball researchers overreached, though, when they snorted that Einstein made little contribution during the second half of his career. *Horsepucky*. The inventor of the *Eee Equals Em Cee Squared* also had a few more gold stars to his reputation, such as:

David Ben-Gurion offered him the presidency of the new state of Israel, but he turned down the offer with great regret. He was also correct to do so, and even this added to his worldwide esteem.

He toured the world for a couple decades, drawing huge crowds who wanted to see a real genius.

He played the violin well enough to give benefit performances. Somehow he fit that into his researches.

He campaigned vigorously with the NAACP for improved rights for black Americans.

He gave high marks to American political laws and traditions, especially for the freedom to speak regardless of social "position."

He proved to be the final push in convincing President Franklin Roosevelt to go ahead with the massive work and funding necessary for the atomic bomb project. We must say that he also very much opposed the widespread use of this weapon by the military, especially against Japan in World War II. In his previous travels, he was much-liked by the Japanese, and he spoke well about them in return.

Near his death, he requested no extraordinary measures to prolong his life, supposedly saying, "I want to go when I want. It is tasteless to prolong life artificially. I have done my share, it is time to go. I will do it elegantly." Indeed. My man.

And that hair. That beautiful hair! When you ask your friends, "Is my hair *einsteining up* today?" then everybody knows exactly what you are asking. If only my gray matter underneath the einsteining-up could expand at the same light speed.

Molière, Patron Saint

This irrepressible and wordy French playwright popularized the term "misanthrope" several centuries ago with his famous play by that name ("Le Misanthrope"). Popularity would not be an item on the top of a real misanthrope's wish list, ironically. For a playwright, though, popularity translates to income and lifeblood. This comedy and most famous of Molière's plays has a fairly straightforward theme, but with the usual seventeenth century twists. Long plays call for several subplots to give customers their money's worth. Briefly, this is that famous story:

Alceste (the misanthrope) rejects the seventeenth century French *uber-politesse* of social conventions. This makes him quite unpopular with others, and sadly introspective with himself. He sees the world as superficial, and his several friends cannot persuade him to act otherwise.

One day he is asked by an acquaintance and powerful member of the nobility, Monsieur Oronte, to judge a sonnet he had just composed honestly. Alceste does *exactly* that. No niceties, no fibbing, he tells Oronte that his poetry is god-awful. For Alcest's uncompromising directness and refusal to go against principle, Oronte has him arrested and sent to trial. Alceste is convicted and humiliated. What a great country!

There are a bunch of women importantly weaving in and out of the story, with all the affections of all the parties typically going toward all the wrong persons. These various love interests do make the story balanced and worthy of good comedy. Alceste at this miserable point decides to exile himself, with friends scurrying off to talk him into coming back at play's end. Sometimes we understand Alceste, but mostly we want to slap sense into the silly French bump-on-a-log.

Alceste clearly did not have the Three Rules for Misanthropes that he needed. He confused bluntness for misanthropy. He cannot be called a misanthrope in our modern sense. If he truly disliked being around mankind, as he claimed, he would have done the real work of telling his sonnet-pleaders what they needed to know (or at least to hear temporarily), rather than simply calling them dummies. With smarter planning like this, M. Oronte would have walked away reasonably pleased, and *never bothered Alceste with his bad poetry again*. Misanthropy contains vast wisdom! Misanthropy requires work!

Was Molière himself a misanthrope? The evidence does not support that, but do let us wait until we can get an original copy of his reality DVD. What seems more likely was that the French government had banned Molière's two previous plays, Tartuffe and Don Juan, and he desperately needed to come up with something good to refill his treasury. "Le Misanthrope" did this spectacularly, at least for theater owners centuries later.

Alceste does give us a few good rules of thumb about the wisdom of *not* blurting out personal criticisms wildly.

• Do not tell a person your honest opinion of his bad hat if the person clearly is in no humor to hear you.

• Ditto, if not involving personal safety. Actually, even if it is.

• Ditto, if the misanthrope himself wants to be somewhere else, or be doing a more interesting project.

Molière's play hands us down many, many good quotations. Some simply observe how humans interact against their best interests:

"One should examine oneself for a very long time before thinking of condemning others."

"Pure reason avoids extremes, and requires one to be wise in moderation."

"The more we love our friends, the less we flatter them; //"It is by excusing nothing that pure love shows itself."

"Things are only worth what one makes them worth."

"Doubts are more cruel than the worst of truths."

"He who establishes his argument by noise and command shows that his reason is weak."

And from *Le Misanthrope* dealing with misanthropy:

"To esteem everything is to esteem nothing."

"Solitude terrifies the soul at twenty."

"Anyone may be an honorable man, and yet write verse badly."

Too bad Alceste did not heed all this good advice, some from himself, or he would not have spoken these lines near the end:

"Betrayed and wronged in everything,
I'll flee this bitter world where vice is king,
And seek some spot unpeopled and apart
Where I'll be free to have an honest heart."

Good verse, bad logic. You'll have an honest heart, and no one around to raw-haw-haw it up over some large beers. Even as this has become Molière's best play, they say he hated how the character Alceste was depicted as a sort of fool on stage. He fervently wanted the audience to agree with Alceste and his views about society.

Well, why didn't you pay attention to how people reacted to those first performances, you old French misanthrope bump-on-a-log!

Poppy's turn now. Enough said....

GOLDEN BOY STRIKES AGAIN

"Gotch'a Last!"

Reinventing Yourself

Technically, cold-bloodedly, reinventing one's self should be easy as snapping the fingers and declaring, "I am hereby reinvented!" Well, maybe becoming a heavyweight world champion Greco-Roman wrestler would take a hair longer for us lighter guys, as long as we have chosen our great-great-grandpa well. Besides, we are talking real Olympic-level work here. How about just reinventing a personal history instead? Spies do it all the time. So do movies.

At a book fair in Maryland I met David Jonathan Sawyer, who authored a really interesting book, "My Great-Grandfather was Stonewall Jackson." (Now sold on Amazon.) Many people claim that same family connection, of course, but what made this story interesting was that the author was quite black. Sometimes in life, inspiration rolls in like a Normandy tide. Clearly, my next book should be, "The Fabulous, Famous Great-Grandson of Frederick Douglass." Me! What makes this otherwise ordinary-sounding claim interesting is that anthropologists would classify me as quite *Caucasoid*.

Why wouldn't my book be any less wild than the one from the guy I just met? What a spectacular way to reinvent myself! Who could top that! Mr. Sawyer and I could also join up and *salt-'n-pepper* the heck out of our joint books, to the great fame of us both! At least we could swap a string of beers at some Baltimore pub.

The first step toward my reinvention as Douglass' heir should be something meaningful, spectacular, and practical: such as joining the local Frederick Douglass Toastmasters club. We do have one in the area. To be candid, I should consider my shortcomings first, so let's play *Compare and Contrast*:

- *Frederick Douglass didn't need no stinkin' speech club.* After some practice, I wouldn't even be fill-in speaker at a local sheep dip manufacturer's club.
- *Frederick Douglass spoke with presidents of the USA about winning wars.* I haven't spoken with a sitting president of the United States at length. Yet. Not even a non-sitting or dead one. Not even a simple "Hello."
- *Frederick Douglass convinced a country to free millions of persons for full citizenship.* I'm still working on that.
- *Frederick Douglass taught himself to read and write, by himself.* I am still trying to teach myself grammar.
- *Frederick Douglass escaped from a bondage situation and make his way through a majority world, most of whom did not like him very much.* I haven't even mastered the skill of escaping from a dull party.

Considering these few humps to overcome, maybe I could work them out with some effort, with a little push. I could work evenings and weekends!

On the other hand, how about just claiming to be the only Romanov descended through the line of W.C. Fields? Sounds easier.

"The Vacuum is Mightier than the Pen"

Don't be silly. Anyway, a person we shall randomly name *Carol* came up with that horrible new proverb one day. Before the telling of the evil deed, though, we need a short unnecessary history about that original more famous proverb.

The "pen vs. the sword" thing got invented by Mister Doctor Baron Edward George Earle Bulwer-Lytton in his 1839 play about French Cardinal Duke Armand Jean du Plessis Richelieu. Serves then both right for getting fathers who gave them long dumb-ass names like that. A few zillion others have claimed credit for that pen & sword proverb, though none ever hit it exactly right until Mr. *Etcetera* Bulwer-Lytton.

Anyway, one day "Carol" demonstrated the ugly new proverb by rolling a military-grade vacuum cleaner head over my organized personal writing area, where ample new drafts and writing materials lay, minding their own bid'ness. This tool was one of those vacuum attachments with tank treads and a cowcatcher, and roaring like a Bremerhaven tramp steamer. None of my stuff got exactly sucked into the vacuum bag, but the papers went through a good scrunch & noogie job. The blue gel pen simply came out disgusting, being covered with old crumbs, a juicy fur ball, and a small pudding spill.

All right, this proved that the pen could be silenced by the vacuum. One time. Just wait until I get new paper, new pen and my old skill writing sarcasm at 30 words per minute. Boy, would the world see my blistering brilliance! The only thing is, all future writing tools would always have to be stashed away, high up somewhere. Besides, nobody would likely buy my story because most of the world would side with the vacuum.

Note: some college stamped the Latin version of "pen vs. the sword" over its door: *Calamus Gladio Fortior*. Over my writing area this "Carol" would change that to: *Electrolux Calamo Fortior*. Good grief! I would at least agree that vacuums suck.

The Reading
(of "The Vacuum is Mightier than the pen")

That *Vacuum* story is true.

No, it isn't. Only partially. See, I did write it and read it out loud to her. I read it to her at a nearby lake park. We had sub sandwiches and I read it to her while we munched. Very romantic. I then asked her if she liked the story.

She loves me, of course. So I sez, "How did all that come out?"

"Great," she sez.

She loves me.

"Well, anything need to be changed?" sez I again.

"Well, yes," she sez, munching, "next time Poppy's sub needs just plain oil-n-vinegar dressing."

Eat, Pray, Text

Y ou see that guy at the next table, head bowed, obviously involved in something other than digging into that last tasty bite of smoked turkey sandwich? You are not trying to be a nosy, judgmental snot when you wonder what the gent is doing. Is he saying belated *grace* for a great lunch? Is he texting one of his often-annoyed buddies? Is he merely calculating his meal tip—a generous one, we hope?

Enough speculating, I say. Here is how you can come up with the correct answer quickly with a little brain work, you nosy, judgmental, speculating snot. Look at the gent's body language. Answer these questions, as Sherlock Holmes would do:

1. Is the gent blinking his eyes?
2. Are his lips moving?
3. Wriggling his elbow-forearm complex?

If the answer to 1 and 2 is "no," but is "yes" to number 3, then he can only be *texting*. Why? Because this combination tell-tales a person's intense concentration. If there was such a thing as physio-sociologists, they would agree: *texting*, by far, takes the most focus of the three activities, no matter how worthless the text of the texting. Moving lips indicate thinking about petition words and grammar for a prayer, or numbers to punch into a calculator, all of which get done ahead of the saying or the computing. Texting, by modern standards, happens faster than a person can *say* or *compute*, making lip movement physically impossible.

Now, some readers will come running up sweating, arm-waving and ranting something about how praying or tip-calculating are certainly *much* more important than texting. Well, probably, but texting wins the *focus* contest, twiddling thumbs down. That explains why the texter *perp* only has riveted eyes for his keypad, no extra time for other unnecessary bodily motions. Witness the hapless, coltish stumbling into mall display fountains, caught on camera, as a good example.

By the way, any kid who thinks his classroom teacher cannot see this texting body language will surely graduate as a first-class knucklehead dumbbell, who would have trouble calculating a lunch tip anyway.

Now a tip for the tip-calculator in this story. His worried, extra bodily movements fumbling around aimlessly on the calculator are completely unnecessary! Because the meal was great, figuring the generous tip will be easy: move the decimal point one place to the left, double the number, and then round it up. Don't be a nosy, judgmental, speculating, preachy snot by telling him so, though.

Mediocrity Trilogy - 1: The Eagle and the Half Cookie

N o, old Aesop never wrote such a tale, not even involving a whole cookie. In fact, the two objects do not connect at all, except in one way: physics.

An eagle glides with Ph.D. expertise through ten jillion air molecules every moment as he soars and dips his very own flight path wherever he wishes. He *don't need no stinkin' air traffic controller* as he slips this way and power floats that way. He circles the skies on his own time, maybe having a sort of working lunch, maybe just playing or winging it. Even a D-student eagle knows how to adjust to the temperatures and pressures of those ten jillion air molecules.

Another lunch happens at the same time on the surface of the earth at an outdoor café. Dessert happens last, and a dry, dreary factory baked chocolate chip cookie gets half tasted, then half tossed into the street nearby. A brief rain soon washes the half cookie down the nearest sewer inlet, and eventually it gets swept along by the hundred jillion water molecules obeying the gravity dictator's rules. A short time later the half cookie finds itself swirling around a giant vortex, following the laws of fluid flow in a gravity system, around and around and around.

Yes, the eagle will die too soon someday. Meanwhile, there's much circling to do. Sometimes it really *is* about lunch, at other times something much more interesting. The eagle flies his adventure, seeing and soaring.

The half cookie does no work at all as it sweeps counterclockwise around the huge cylindrical drain.

Actually, the water *itself* does herculean work, say the physicists. Unless the half cookie tries a backstroke, though, it does none. But, the scenery isn't *all* bad. The shiny glint from the steel drain wall could be looked at as a silver lining in the cloudy water, occasionally glimpsed.

Which one *wins*—the eagle slowly wearing his wing feathers to death from self-propelled adventure, or a patch of soggy crumbs circling the drain?

Mediocrity Trilogy - 2: Circling the Drain

W hat a scary phrase. The *average* brain usually thinks, "Uh, oh, Yer' gonna' die." No, no, not really, says NY financial advisor/analyst and columnist Charles Payne. It is not so much about *death*, as it is about spiraling downward to *mediocrity*, he explains.

Now, Mr. Payne has spent much of his valuable, limited daily column space over the past decade pounding the podium about the evils of settling for mediocrity. Not only *settling* in large, national and financial matters, but also (and especially) in an individual's daily personal choices. Since his firm has a rare reputation for prediction accuracy, we could afford to listen a little longer than the 30-second average attention span.

After a good half year's reading his columns, I mostly get it: mediocrity is worse than "butt ugly." Right-o. This hatred of mediocrity ranges from big banks not doing their job (lending), to persons cutting corners day to day (living). Now, let this amateur gremlin summarize the point of view in a meat-and-potatoes way.

First, though, "mediocre" does not mean "average." *Average* could be a mostly respectable word (except maybe for "low average attention span"). Don't you suspect that large companies would kill to have everyone in the company *please* just perform at "average level"! Heck, if that half cookie circling the sewer tank could just do an *average* backstroke, it would get a standing ovation.

All right, then, *Mediocrity Case 1: Dirty-sock Coffee.* Mediocrity might be more like settling for a restaurant that uses luke-warm water to brew your 6 AM coffee. How happy would your taste bud tissues be with that tepid swill coming its way? (If your name is *Luke*, neither connection nor offense meant; please buy this book, Cool Hand Luke.) Anyway, mediocrity by "settling" gets you something like early morning coffee resembling shredded brown crayons filtered through yesterday's dish rag.

Mediocrity Case 2: The Glass Card Table. How much fun would it be winning a round of solitaire if you do so by peeking *under* the table—for the forty-third time? Cripes, running a bank or a life like a glass-table card game cheater? Forget about *psychology*, just work smarter!

Mediocrity Case 3: Waiting for Godot. "He that waits upon fortune is never sure of a dinner," quoth Benjamin Franklin. Dr. Franklin did not say that *hope is an excuse for today*, but it means the same thing. You know those zillion-dollar power lotteries? They aren't gambling—you *aren't* going to win.

These Cases are funny enough, but anyone settling for swill? So, waiting for the lottery to cough up, we head for the drain, circling the tank.

Mediocrity Trilogy - 3: Swimming with the Fishes/Tank

T his fish story came from somewhere real, I'm sure, and certainly from the middle of 20th Century Britain. To get started, let's say it was told by English businessman Ian Clive Aesop from Westwebstershropshire (pronounced "Wesshirr").

There was this English frozen fish startup company that snagged its catches from the Mediterranean. The first fish tank shipment returned home with—what turned out to be—a tasteless end product.

The brilliant staff marine biologist MBA spotted the problem right away. "The fish are not moving," he pontificated. True enough, it seems. After capture, the fish sat listlessly in the tank, exerting themselves next to zero, maybe twitching their caudal fins once every two minutes to stay more or less stationary. As fisherpersons say, "One spot is as good as another." No exertion means no fish juices flowing vigorously through the fish. No fish juices flowing means tasteless fish dinners later. Customers want *swell* fish, not *swill*.

The company's brilliant staff engineer then designed and installed a giant paddle in the fish tank to create a current to stir the fish around. The moving water would be a sort of motivational seminar for the fish. Alas, the end product turned out to be almost tasteless, again. On investigation, the fish still merely floated listlessly in the fake current that swirled them furiously around. What to do now? What to do?

Then a brilliant company dock worker and amateur fisherperson piped up. "Toss a small shark in the bloody tank." That worked. The predator put enough natural incentive into the fish to keep their juices flowing, vigorously. One assumes that the company only used a few such predators, perhaps only one, which also had a small appetite along with large teeth. No point in needlessly whittling down the company's capital stock.

Well now, isn't that just great? All this big talk about using personal energy to overcome mediocrity, and your swimming fish get eaten in the end. That's the point? What kind of inspiration does that amount to, Mr. Big Writer, Mr. Big Smartie-britches Writer!

Well, all right, the fish get eaten. And, we will all die someday. We *will* all die someday. In that time gap before then, would it not be much better to make life juicier, more *accomplishful*, mainly for oneself? Certainly the actively swimming fish in the large tank with the small predator are more pleased with their life. Aren't they? Sounds like a sterling Ph.D. research topic. Let's not give it that third degree, though, and just say that at least these sea creatures really could do a respectable and vigorous backstroke, unlike that patch of cookie crumbs sloshing down the sewer drain.

DISCLAIMER: NO EAGLES, COOKIES, FISH, VEGANS, ENGLISHMEN, ENGINEERS, MBAs, OR LUKES WERE HARMED IN THE PRODUCTION OF THESE TALES.

The Logic of Coincidences

This could be short: there *isn't* any logic. You just get lucky or unlucky from time to time. But to make a very short story *longer*....

There was a trendy book on the topic of biorhythms, published sometime in the 1970s, where the author explained how you should avoid certain physical and mental activities on your "biorhythm down days." He tells how President John Kennedy, on one of his *personal down days,* threw out his back at a local groundbreaking ceremony, shoveling dirt or something. Why, didn't he know better? How foolish could he have been, for *petey's* sake? If he was so rich & powerful, how come he wasn't smart! Yes, the author chugged out a whole book on all that biorhythm theory stuff. Judging by its popularity at the time, he also chugged all the way to his bank, often.

Each of three major biorhythm cycles is supposed to go from "personal low" to "personal high," then back again to low in a 20-30 day range, each cycle having slightly different length (*real* scientists say, "period"). Therefore, every adult of Kennedy's fortyish age has to have gone through about 600 of these twenty-plus-day cycles in his or her life by that time.

Can the thinking person believe that only *one* of those 600 bad spots in the cycles had to be a bad-shovel day for the president? In truth, I forgot which of President K.'s three biorhythms had dipped down, but it must have been a biggie. Maybe even all three. What a coincidence!

Here is a nonscientific thought about all that. If you get *enough* examples of *enough* days from *enough* famous persons over *enough* years, it might just be possible to show how one of them messed up by being dumb with a shovel on a biorhythm down day. *After the fact*, that is. The heck with *beforehand* predictions. Also, how come we do not know if President Kennedy didn't mess his back up during one of those 599 other times? I'll bet my smart readers (all of you) figured this out even before I said it. It may not be important or connected, but you will also recall that President Kennedy never had a *bad-hair* day, even lolling in the Pacific Ocean off the side of sunken PT-109.

Time for a personal story. I give you a clue about the topic: Clue! Everyone living through the heady days of board games knows Clue. The rules to this excellent time-waster go like this:

• The game board displays the top view of a really, really expensive mansion, whose owner just got himself bumped-off dead.

• Players have to guess which of the possible characters was the *perp*, what room he/she did the murder, and with which of the possible weapons he/she used.

• Players roll dice to move around the mansion.

• When a player arrives at a room, he/she can ask questions of other players to get—aha!—*clues* about the crime.

• By elimination of false clues, eventually someone can guess—"Make the Accusation"—about the crime details, and if correct, he/she wins.

Clue plays sort of like a mixture of Candyland, craps, and Old Maid.

As a wee kid, playing Clue the first time, I accused *Mr. Green* of bonking the victim with the *lead pipe* in the *Conservatory*. Correctly, without even using all those Clues worksheets. What a coincidence! Not being able to spell "deduce," much less use it in a complete sentence, this UNprecocious brat somehow got it right. How could this happen? Of course it was a coincidence!

Consider this, though: Mr. Green's picture on the game box looked like a thieving, skulking killer to me. The conservatory room in the mansion had this neat secret passageway to another room. And the lead pipe was the only murder weapon token that was soft and bendy.

The rest of the family wondered about my cleverness. I knew I was just lucky. Coincidences *can* happen once in a while, coincidentally.

The Grass Is Geezer on the Other Side

Does anyone else know that "geezer" was defined as an old *woman* in a late 1800s dictionary? Yeah. How %#$@&#&^!! sexist can a dictionary be?

Nowadays most persons think of "geezer" as an older, not necessarily wiser, *man*. Geez, how sexism has swapped itself in a short century! %#$@&#&^!!

Remember how we said "*geezertude* must be earned" in the Einstein story earlier (p. 196)? Well, this is pure, naked truth, without making people mad by getting naked. Think how hard it is to get older, how much experience has to get used up and blown, how many meals have to be wolfed, how many steins of beer—good and not so much—have to get quaffed. Think how many muscle and non-muscle groups need constant movement. All of this and much more is just plain bald hard work.

Now think of the pros that come with becoming a professional geezer:

• You could get up in the morning when you *durn* well please.

• You can fix your breakfast using any (or none) of the 17 major food groups to concoct it.

• You can enjoy concocting the mess at your own speed (but very savvy to clean up at your kitchen partner's speed).

• You can loll over your splendid self-prepared concoction at your own pace.

• You can plan your day, or week, or remaining lifetime in any non-prescribed, non-military manner. Note that the first two time spans stay pretty much constant, but that third one (lifetime) does get easier by virtue of getting shorter every passing hour.

 • Last, you can bore into your planning at tunnel-mining speed, or at loll speed, or you can just bag the whole thing and drop into the Wildcat Gentlemen's Establishment for the afternoon.

You see? The grass is always, always greener over the next fence when you have nearly 100% choice about that grass on the other side. You can stomp on it, water it, or Round-Up® the whole shebang. As long as you find yourself physically standing there looking at it, you *haven't* got a problem. The grass is always *geezer*, savvy old-timers!

A Donkey on I-95

S peaking of the U.S. National Defense and Interstate Highway System, I-95 from Maine to Florida separates Americans into two groups. The first consists of all the folks who have been treated to a drive along this massive east-coast interstate. The second is those who are still awaiting the treat.

I-95 has only one problem, but it's a big one. That is the congestion, randomly scattered along its massive north-south length. Picture dipping a long fuzzy string into a jar of honey. The sticky stuff pretty much gloms itself over the string in random spots, top to bottom, and hangs on like three chimps on a backpack of ripe bananas. I-95 can have sticky "bubbles" of congestion during rush hours at, say, places like New York City, Trenton, Philadelphia, Baltimore, Washington DC, Fredericksburg (VA), and Richmond. Make that during lunch hours also. But, no need to anger more loyal I-95-city hometown readers of this good book.

Speaking of traffic congestion, some expert said that if average interstate speed is at least 30 mph, then it's better to *stay on* the interstate, rather than cutting onto the side roads to save time[1].

What if the congestion at those many I-95 *glom* points causes speeds lower than 30 mph, though? Much, much slower. Would not an old geezer on a donkey, with donkey-driving skills, offering donkey connecting rides be a fabulous time saver to the smart commuter? For a small fee, say, a dollar a pound, the donkey can get a person past the interstate congestion

---

1. I forget who said this and when he said it, or where it got printed, but this fake footnote might keep the lawsuits down.

faster than an automobile can. The donkey's fuel is completely biodegradable on the way in and on the way out.

Speaking of geezers, yes, the old rider-donkey-driver also has personal parts that glom up and slow down, grind or simply hurt. Pole vaulting twenty feet now becomes an impossibility, at least under existing rules. Some of these unfortunate changes can be fixed, or at least medicated, but so what? The poor donkey does the walking part of this big program. Both donkey and geezer at first seem obsolete, but brilliant ideas never are.

At the end of all this you must know that I-95 is an old revered workhorse too. In spite of the honey-cluster congestion points glommed along the way, this workhorse-machine gets people long, long distances fast on the average. By himself, a donkey would have a hard time doing the whole distance with one feed bag and one old aching donkey-express rider. I-95 really is a machine, when you think about it, and probably one of the largest ones in the world.

Speaking of this Big Donkey Movement, the program will likely not catch on. Part of the reason has to do with the piling up of heaps of donkey movement on the interstate shoulder after a week or two. Although this would cut down on the number of commuters pulling off the road to make a call, change a tire, or eat their breakfast pizza, the cops would have the donkeys in cuffs pretty quickly. These good public servant pros don't put up with much crap.

Free Range Geezer

> "Cussing is when you say bad words about something or someone, or when you stub your toe. Cursing is the same thing, only in complete sentences."

G reat-great grandpa supposedly said this a couple centuries ago after delivering a speech at one of those lively Scottish town meetings. Being a member of the opposition, and always a smart-aleck, he had likely already stirred the ire of the majority by rising and asking questions, i.e., irritating the majority. He must have survived the meeting, because *I* am here. Great-great grandpa decided to leave for America, becoming my Great Model for a true free range geezer.

Think of a free range chicken. This animal enjoys popularity these days, at least after baking. Credit this to ideas such as freedom to travel, freedom to eat whatever foods the chicken finds natural and healthful, freedom to exercise (or not), depending on what seems "good" to the chicken himself. A free range geezer is sort of like all that, only doesn't get served with dumplings at the end.

Great-great grandpa decided to chase these freedoms, knowing that he would have to use his brains and his patience to get to, and then thrive in this new America. He had to use smarts to know when to move and be bold, and when to keep his mouth shut. This must have worked, because *I* am here.

Great-great grandpa likely also participated in his American town meetings, but did not repeat his preachy "cuss" remark. Although the people down south (where he ended up) liked him well enough, he spoke with that brogue, so they probably thought he was somehow cussing anyway. Every scrap of work or play he did, and his every thought must have reflected the free range of his natural person, and of his new adopted country.

The best I might hope for myself, in keeping with my ancestor's strong personality, is an epitaph like, "He was last seen chasing the sunset on I-90 in his old car, cussing at the accelerator." Thank you, Great-great grandpa.

> *It's been really fun. The next acknowledgment speaks for itself*

EPILOGGING OUT

Tales of Steven

So.... The reader will recall that weird publisher caper which started out this whole *shebang*. At some point, the smarter and older author will finally realize that he needs a second opinion. Badly. On just about everything, from the picking of topics to using incomplete sentences. At the end of this long story, then, Poppy charged straight over to that second publisher, whom we shall call "Steven." His name is almost certainly a business pseudonym which his parents gave him at birth. Here's how this happy story really happened.

"What's this about your riding a lawn mower to see that publisher over yonder, Poppy?" Steven asks, dangling some conversational bait.

"Must be an old farmer's tale," Poppy mutters, "but might be a good story to add somewhere in this manuscript thing in front of you."

"All right. Why don't you read me a couple of the pieces you wrote," sez Steven tolerantly.

"Out loud?" the old goat sez, taken aback.

"Well, that beats chanting 'ohmmm' and telepathing the stuff. My antennas probably couldn't pick up the syntax anyway," continues Publisher Number Two, "so read on, MacDuff."

"Okie dokie. that *Mein Geezer* thing, where this whole project started...."

For some fine reason, Steven listens calmly. Occasionally he tosses a conversational dart like, "Was that ungrammatical phrase done on purpose?" Et cetera. Actually, virtual critique darts fly often. Talk then turns to heavier matters.

You see, authors have a long history of ignoring the inconvenient parts of getting a book from desktop to the B&N shelf, such as how to sell this stack of paper pages with a bunch of ink scribbled in the middle, and with a cover glued onto one end. Being a kind sort, Steven then cordially suggests doing many, many public readings. He also recommends looking around for professional editing help with the *manuscript*—the writing world still uses this medieval monkish noun.

Looking back, it did not sound like Steven worried much about the book's final title wording, as he thought this half-happy oddball in front of him might have more pressing problems to tend to. He said something helpful about how this whole deal gets easier after a dozen readings or so, and talked about a string of other suggestions, without mentioning the minor possibility of just *bagging* the whole thing.

Sheeeesh!

He was quite right, of course, to his point that *nothing* in this universe gets done—especially writing and selling a book—unless the hard work gets finished. All of it. He also warned Poppy about not waving his arms around like some clumsy, inarticulate boob when doing public readings. Steven is an especially valuable Golden Gremlin.

> *Steven, please just sign off now and close your ears....*

ASSORTED INAPPROPRIATE SONGS

Auld Lang Sigh

Make new friends,

And ke-ep the-ee old:

One is sil-ver,

And the other is BALD.

Dance of the Sugarplum Prïi

Backing out,
creep,
roll,
stop.
Prius go
ever slow,
boring show,
cars with stubby snout...
Back me out once more ---

Top of hill,
roll,
down,
roll,
common gripe,
overhype,
racing stripe,
never get that thrill...
Pedal to the floor ---

Bat-ter-y
big,
weight,
slow,
can't go far,
pudgy car,
falling star,
got no flattery...
No plug for sad Eeyore ---

gas
low....

Take Me Out to the Bald Game

Take me out to the bald game

Take me to my slick crowd,

Buy me a comb and minoxidil,

I don't care if I'm over the hill.

Oh it's roots, roots, roots in the bathtub,

Get me my brush just the same,

For it's one, two, three strokes it's gone

In the old bald game.

O Holiday Tree

O Holiday Tree, O Holiday Tree,
Here comes that dog to water thee.
O Holiday Tree, O Holiday Tree,
I'd shoot that mutt with greatest glee:
Every day he passes by,
Circles 'round and let's 'er fly.
O Holiday Tree, O Holiday Tree,
How brown thy leaves are going to be!

O Holiday Tree, O Holiday Tree,
Doggie wet thy branches.
O Holiday Tree, O Holiday Tree,
We'll fry him as he prances:
A hidden strand of 'lectric wire
Turn the switch-'n set-'is hose on fire,
O Dead-dog Tree, O Dead-dog Tree,
You're now both brown and crispy.

Omega
Man
Press

ORDER FORM

_____ **GOLDEN GREMLIN**, $13.95 US ($10.95 US/ea. for qty 5+).

Other books by Rod A. Walters:

_____ **TOXIC ASSETS**, $13.95 US ($8.95 US/ea. for quantity 5+).

_____ **PENNY, PASSED BY**. $8.95 US ($4.95 US/ea. for 5+).

_____ **A SOLDIER'S PAY**. $8.95 US ($4.95 US/ea. for 5+).

_____ **SILVER**. $6.95 US ($3.95 US/ea. for 5+).

Fax orders: 585-271-6065
Telephone orders: 585-451-5557
Email orders: info@ieWriter.com
U.S. Mail orders: OMEGA MAN PRESS, 30 Wilmington Street S-302, Rochester, NY 14620. Shipping: $2.00 first book, $1.00 for each additional.

Name: _____

Address: _____

City: _____ State:_____ Zip:_____

Telephone: _____

Email address: _____

Sales Tax: Please add 8.0% for books shipped to NY addresses.
Shipping by air, U.S.: $6.00 US for first book, $2.50 US for each additional.
Shipping by air, International.: $12.00 US for first book, $6.00 US for each additional.

89013695R00128

Made in the USA
Columbia, SC
16 February 2018